MADLY Marvelous

MADLY Marvelous

THE COSTUMES OF

BY DONNA ZAKOWSKA

To my mother and all women
who strive to surround themselves
with beauty in spite of all

Table of Contents

FOREWORD

by Amy Sherman-Palladino

It's time to bring back Pink." Donna Zakowska stood in her studio on the third floor of Steiner Studios, a magic room of hats and shoes and skirts and gloves, dressed all in black, like a ninja, explaining the reasoning behind her proclamation. Midge's coat in the pilot was pink. In the pilot she was with Joel. When they broke up, the pink was gone. But now that Midge seems to be finding her way forward again—we're bringing back pink. Of course it will be a different pink, because she's a different girl, but it will be pink.

Pink tells a story.

The Marvelous Mrs. Maisel is the show I have been waiting my whole life to do. I wanted it to be a big show. I wanted to revisit the New York that I had heard about from my parents. To bring to life the tales of the Greenwich Village basket houses and the Catskills hotels my father worked at as a stand-up comic. And to accomplish this task I needed several things: unbreakable actors, the crew of the gods, production design conjured by wizards—and costumes. Marvelous, beautiful costumes. Costumes that move and dance.

Costumes that tell a story.

So into my life walked a tiny woman who would haunt my dreams. And my stories.

Donna Zakowska is uncompromising. Her designs are specific and there's a reason for every button, every pocket. Everything must be perfect. And not just for our star, Rachel Brosnahan, or our leading actors, but for every single person on our show. She marches up and down the lines of extras, sometimes hundreds of them, inspecting every detail, correcting every flaw, for every scene we do. "Button that." "Don't take the hat off, I told you that." "You have gloves? Where are your gloves?" "What's in your pocket? Why? I don't care if it's your life-saving medication, it's ruining the line of your suit. Throw it out." Okay, the last one never happened, but it could. And frankly she would be right.

Nothing escapes her eye. She's a perfectionist's perfectionist. For Miami she created a sort of bubble sun romper, inspired by some pictures of Miami in the fifties, that looked like beach balls with great legs walking around on the beach. Ridiculous and fabulous. She makes costumes that are dreamy, funny, sexy, insane . . . everything that I need this show to be.

Her clothes can be frilly, flirty, sad, or defiant. There are coats that feel like superhero capes and hats that feel like crowns or cherries on top of a sundae. And every one of them is like nothing you've ever seen before.

I have given Donna many nicknames over the last five years. My two favorites being "Generale" and "Genius." And because she is a professional, and a cool lady, she has tolerated these nicknames with a mixture of bewilderment and probably a little annoyance. But hopefully she understands they are meant with great love, affection, and admiration.

And quite a bit of gratitude for giving her all . . . to help me tell my story.

INTRODUCTION

by Donna Zakowska

I grew up with my mother and grandmother in an old nineteenth-century house in Vinegar Hill, Brooklyn, regularly descended upon by a bevy of Italian aunts, at the center of a constant flurry of social events and holiday celebrations. And my mother embraced each change of season and holiday as if decorating and dressing for the occasion were essential obligations of daily life. The house was decked with metallic silver icicles in the winter, then red velvet roses, tulips in the spring, autumn leaves and pumpkins in the fall. It sometimes felt like living in a giant window display, with heaps of fabric flowers and ornament boxes in constant rotation from the basement.

Amidst the various household decorations, my mother also regularly conjured up boxes of clothing and hats, and I took particular pleasure in donning my grandmother's vintage clothing. My mother was an unwavering believer in the power of adornment—and the idea that, whatever the circumstances of one's life, one should never abandon the commitment to beautification and embellishment, either of one's surroundings or oneself.

On one of my first films, Carl Franklin's *One True Thing*, my mother's guiding principle was very much in my thoughts when I was designing the costumes for Meryl Streep's character, Kate, who was diagnosed with cancer and unwilling to succumb to its effect on her outward appearance. We created a wardrobe rich in holiday clothing and accessories—like Christmas corsages and sweaters—with attractive, uplifting details to express her unrelenting celebration of daily life in the face of adversity. The headscarves she wore in the aftermath of her cancer treatments were made from very special Italian silks and wools, and I remember being amazed by the number of women who reached out to me afterward wanting to find these scarves for themselves—an affirmation, I thought, of my mother's belief.

Years later, then, in one of my first meetings with the creator and producers of *The Marvelous Mrs. Maisel*, I heard another strong echo of my mother's constant credo, when, in describing the show's main character, Midge, Amy Sherman-Palladino declared that whatever took place in her life, we would never portray the *marvelous* Mrs. Maisel as despondent or defeated. And so, the creation of the world of *Mrs. Maisel*, with its effusion of accessories and color, often transported me back to my childhood experience of the transformational power of adornment and its equation with self-esteem . . .

I am therefore first and foremost grateful to Amy and her accomplice, Dan Palladino—both for having the genius to conceive of the show and for asking me to join them on their journey.

And to everyone at Amazon who made the journey possible.

And to everyone on the production who gave it life—in particular, producer Dhana Gilbert and her supportive staff; cinematographer M. David Mullen and his crew; and production designer Bill Groom and his art department, with whom I undoubtedly share a psychic link.

And to the entire cast, principals and extras alike, who, after putting up with my mania for minutiae, gave life to the clothes in giving life to their characters.

And to my own assistants and the many other members of my team, too numerous to mention individually, for their various contributions to the costumes, from design to execution to fitting and dressing.

And to all of the independent costume shops that keep the entertainment world humming, among them my most regular collaborators on *Mrs. Maisel*—in New York, Eric Winterling, Donna Langman Costumes, Lynne Mackey Studio, Giliberto Designs, Timberlake Studios; and in Paris, Atelier Caraco.

And to Abrams, for approaching me with the idea for a book about the costumes and then staying the course through the COVID-19 pandemic.

And to the various people who gave so generously of their time above and beyond the call of duty—especially, from the production, Tiffany Parker and Mark Pollard; from my own team, Matthew Caprotti and Ben Philipp; and on behalf of Amazon, Jamie Kampel and Tiffany Shinn.

And to my literary agent, Chris Tomasino, for guiding me through the baby steps of publishing, and my good friend Nion McEvoy from Chronicle Books for connecting us.

To Camille Coy and Sam Jay Gold for their help with graphics and photo editing, and Judith P. for her input and advice on textual matters.

And finally, to my scrivening ghost and overall partner in crime, Roman Paska.

Made to Marvel

CHAPTER 01

The Madly Marvelous Paintbox

*"I knew, from the moment I held the box
of colors in my hand, this was my life."*
—HENRI MATISSE

*"The best color in the whole world is
the one that looks good on you."*
—COCO CHANEL

As a child my favorite plaything was my "painting box." And the great passion of my life has been playing with color—like a cook or a chemist, mixing, testing, measuring, distilling, refining—convinced there's something undeniably magical in the creation and experience of color. After studying painting for many years, from the Brooklyn Museum Art School to the Paris École des Beaux-Arts, my childhood passion ultimately led to a life in costume design, and then—serendipitously!—the development of a madly marvelous paintbox for *The Marvelous Mrs. Maisel*.

LIVING COLOR

Fabric in *The Marvelous Mrs. Maisel* was like pigment for me, and walls and walls of swatches filled the studio as the concoction of a palette for each episode became an intense, intoxicating process. And as I deepened my research into the 1950s, I encountered a use of color in the photography and, by extension, magazines of the period that was explosive and exciting, accompanied by a similarly amazing proliferation of sculptural forms. It was as if, after two major wars, the design world was emerging from a long period of darkness literally breathing shape and color. A whole new spirit of optimism energized clothing design in ways that were perfectly suited to the spirit of *Mrs. Maisel*, the essence of which I hoped to be able to capture in the costumes of the show.

When designing a period project, I always surround myself with historical research material, in this case piles of magazines and photographs from the late 1940s through early 1960s. And I continually steep myself in inspiration from nature since botanical details often subtly infiltrate my designs. I will often find myself focusing on an image of a plant for its potential to suggest a beautiful hat shape—or provide a perfect palette for a sundress in the Catskills! So many costume elements in the series were inspired by natural forms . . .

I also spend a great deal of time poring through other, miscellaneous images, primarily fine art paintings and prints or fragments of graphic design, with a predilection for images from other periods or places that I feel in some way align with the sensibility of the period I'm designing—in this case, late 1950s New York. In fact, I love combining very specific period details with elements from more unexpected, unpredictable sources, convinced that there are no bounds to where inspiration, especially color inspiration, can arise.

BEHIND THE SCHEMES

I've always felt that colors have history, and that, as costume designers, creating clothes as color "events" is our special way of painting the story as we develop a narrative for each character. In designing the clothing for Midge, Mrs. Maisel herself, played by Rachel Brosnahan, I often used color to depict her emotional landscape and give emphasis to moments in which she needed to be particularly comic or heroic or even provocative. . . . So, over the course of season one, from her first pink coat and dress on the Upper West Side to the formal black cocktail dress she wore for her stage debut as "Mrs. Maisel," the costumes plot a chromatic arc that mirrors her emotional trajectory from the world of the would-be happy '50s housewife to the start of her professional career.

And in addition to the principal actors, for me it's just as important to consider how the extras' background palette can contribute to the overall look of each scene.

I continually discuss the projected color schemes with my team of costume fitters, and we create boards and charts with color samples and swatches for extras very much as we do for principals. Each scene, then, has a specific color program—like Midge's wedding party in the pilot, which was dominated by pale floral colors with accents of green like a giant flower bouquet, or the Copacabana audience in episode 104, a study in vibrant, sensual reds, pinks, and blacks.

Color inspiration can either come from a combination of weighty sources or from a single small, seemingly insignificant item or detail. Whether at Steiner Studios, our home base, or on location, our wardrobe world is always crowded with shelves and tables covered with a rainbow array of hats, gloves, shoes, and handbags, since accessories are an important way to enhance or complete the palette of any outfit. And often, in fact, an accessory with a particularly interesting color or pattern will function as the catalyst for a whole costume.

The Marvelous Mrs. Maisel

CHARACTER: 1. MIDGE
ACTOR: RACHEL BROSNAHAN

SWATCH	SWATCH	SWATCH

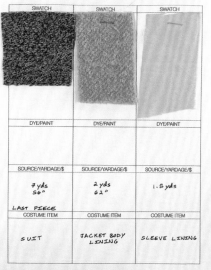

PANTONE 667 U PANTONE 66..

*OVERDYED TO SWATCH

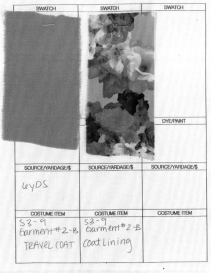

SOURCE/YARDAGE/$	SO...	

COSTUME ITEM	COSTUME ITEM	COSTUME ITEM
PERKY SLEEVELESS DRESS		

The Marvelous Mrs. Maisel

CHARACTER: MIDGE
ACTOR: RACHEL BROSNAHAN

SOURCE/YARDAGE/$	SOURCE/YARDAGE/$	SOURCE/YARDAGE/$
3YRDS	3YRDS	RJ 1284 34YDS

COSTUME ITEM	COSTUME ITEM	COSTUME ITEM
S3-15 #10 BOATING TOP	S3-13 #10 BOATING TOP	S3-13 #11 CAPRI PANTS

The Marvelous Mrs. Maisel

CHARACTER: MIDGE
ACTOR: Rachel Brosnahan

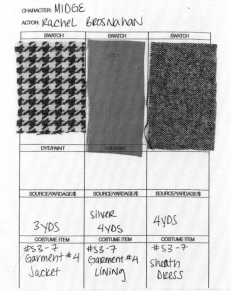

SWATCH	SWATCH	SWATCH

DYE/PAINT	DYE/PAINT	DYE/PAINT

SOURCE/YARDAGE/$	SOURCE/YARDAGE/$	SOURCE/YARDAGE/$
3YDS	SILVER 4YDS	4YDS

COSTUME ITEM	COSTUME ITEM	COSTUME ITEM
#S3-7 Garment #4 Jacket	#S3-7 Garment #4 Lining	#S3-7 Sheath Dress

---

The Marvelous Mrs. Maisel

CHARACTER: MIDGE MAISEL
ACTOR: RACHEL BROSNAHAN

SWATCH	SWATCH	SWATCH

DYE/PAINT	DYE/PAINT	DYE/PAINT

SOURCE/YARDAGE/$	SOURCE/YARDAGE/$	SOURCE/YARDAGE/$
7 yds 56" LAST PIECE	2 yds 62"	1.5 yds

COSTUME ITEM	COSTUME ITEM	COSTUME ITEM
SUIT	JACKET BODY LINING	SLEEVE LINING

The Marvelous Mrs. Maisel

CHARACTER: MIDGE MAISEL
ACTOR: RACHEL BROSNAHAN

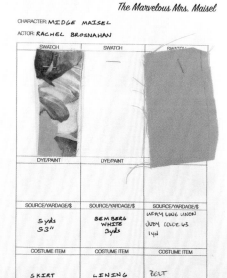

SWATCH	SWATCH	SWATCH

DYE/PAINT	DYE/PAINT	

SOURCE/YARDAGE/$	SOURCE/YARDAGE/$	SOURCE/YARDAGE/$
5 yds S3"	BEMBERG WHITE 3yds	WEARY LINING LINEN JUDY COLOR 63 1yd

COSTUME ITEM	COSTUME ITEM	COSTUME ITEM
SKIRT	LINING	BELT

The Marvelous Mrs. Maisel

CHARACTER: MIDGE
ACTOR: Rachel Brosnahan

SWATCH	SWATCH	SWATCH

DYE/PAINT	DYE/PAINT	

SOURCE/YARDAGE/$	SOURCE/YARDAGE/$	SOURCE/YARDAGE/$
2 yds	4 yds	

COSTUME ITEM	COSTUME ITEM	COSTUME ITEM
TOP	SKIRT	

The Marvelous Mrs. Maisel

CHARACTER: MIDGE
ACTOR: Rachel Brosnahan

SWATCH	SWATCH	SWATCH

		DYE/PAINT

SOURCE/YARDAGE/$	SOURCE/YARDAGE/$	SOURCE/YARDAGE/$
6YDS		

COSTUME ITEM	COSTUME ITEM	COSTUME ITEM
S3-9 Garment #2-B TRAVEL COAT	S3-9 Garment #2-B Coat Lining	

The Marvelous Mrs. Maisel

CHARACTER: MIDGE
ACTOR: Rachel Brosnahan

SWATCH	SWATCH	SWATCH

		DYE/PAINT

SOURCE/YARDAGE/$	SOURCE/YARDAGE/$	SOURCE/YARDAGE/$
6YDS	GIZA CORAL 2YDS	

COSTUME ITEM	COSTUME ITEM	COSTUME ITEM
S3-9 Garment #8 DRESS	S3-9 Garment #8 Bodice Lining	Wide Gold Belt

---

The Marvelous Mrs. Maisel

CHARACTER: MIDGE
ACTOR: Rachel Brosnahan

SWATCH	SWATCH	SWATCH

SOURCE/YARDAGE/$	SOURCE/YARDAGE/$	SOURCE/YARDAGE/$
8YDS 79-	CDC col. 037 8 YRDS	PV3000 ORGANZA 8YRDS col. 114

COSTUME ITEM	COSTUME ITEM	COSTUME ITEM
S3-17 #5 BRIS DRESS	DRESS LINING	POSSIBLE SKIRT UNDERLAYER *NOT SURE IF USED

COLORATURA

I like to think of the palette as a living thing, and in order to remain sensitive to its organic evolution as an ever-present element in the design, we surround ourselves in the studio with all of the clothes we've built, especially for Midge and the other principals. They are organized more by color than chronology—with racks for blue dresses, green, pink. . . . In the case of Midge's outfits, their proximity helps me keep in mind the essence of every scene or state of mind that she was going through when she wore a particular color. So, because the green dress she wore to the precinct house in the pilot was a "heroic" choice, she subsequently wears a green coat at the Washington Square demonstration where she becomes a spontaneous voice for women's rights.

Often, to map the progression of color through the series, I create schematic charts with tiny swatches or dabs of paint. I think of this as an equivalent to notating music or dance since it enables me to track the rhythms and patterns of my choices like musical phrases or movement motifs. Like music, color always has a subliminal effect, and it can transform our immediate, often superficial reactions to a character in unexpected ways. Color truly helps us to connect with our characters' inner lives. . . . And enables us to join them on their journey.

CHAPTER 02

The Madly Marvelous Studio

"Clothes and clothes and more clothes.
Who in Manhattan has a room
entirely full of shoes and purses?"
—ABE

Our madly marvelous studio is equal parts workshop, atelier, research facility, office, library, treasury, armory, depot, kitchen, and lab (!)—both a concept space, because ideas are born there, and a concrete space, because costumes are actually made there.

I start each season conceptually, then, covering virtually every available surface with visual sources to create an immersive environment for myself and my staff where we can steep ourselves in the images and ideas that will play a part in the season, a kind of picture gallery-cum-library consisting of research boards, palette boards, walls of swatches from past and present seasons—and, of course, the books and magazines, period and contemporary, that provide historical background and inspiration. This is particularly important during the early part of prep, before the scripts are finalized, when we might have only the time of year and a few locations to go on—say, springtime in Paris! And it is, in fact, my favorite time in the studio, when I can browse creatively through the research I've collected, noting what inspires me and organizing my thoughts about what I'm hoping to accomplish with the design.

"You're going to need a lot of closet space." —ABE

I also begin by collecting real period prototypes—whole garments or bits and pieces of vintage clothing that then become references for patterns and construction. We never seem to have enough space or surfaces, as tables start overflowing with choice colored felts, buttons, and trims we've found in vintage shops or flea markets. Then, as the script details become more specific, we carefully winnow our stockpile into a tangible visual archive, organizing our research materials into the many receptacles that surround us in the studio for creative stimulation.

The design part of the studio is the nerve center of the department, where, with a core team of assistants, I sketch, assemble, and organize each episode's growing collection of looks. I often refer to it as our costume kitchen or lab because we never stop experimenting with ideas for designs, both on paper and as sculptural forms, and because we're always testing the limits of new and more ambitious possibilities. I keep most of the principals' costumes on racks nearby, including Midge's full wardrobe, both because it inspires me to be able to glance up and be reminded of the variety of colors and shapes that have already been created, and helps maintain continuity in the direction of each season's new designs.

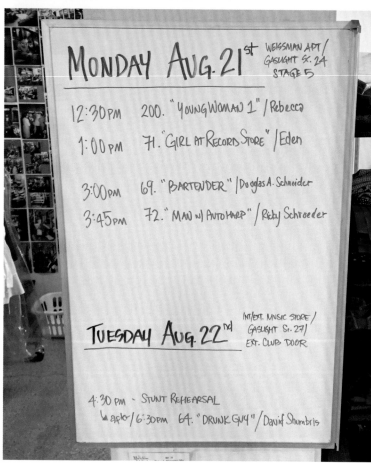

"Have you worn all these dresses?"
—*ABE*

Next door is a room for our in-house tailors and sewers and builders. In general, the principals' clothing is made specifically for the production—either at established costume shops around New York City or in our studio, or for certain specialized items, Europe—as are most of the more theatrical costumes for day players and extras, like the dresses, head-dresses, and jewelry for the Copacabana dancers in season one or the Miami Cuban club dancers in season three—the kind of inventive costumes I especially love to design!

Another large part of the studio is dedicated to fittings and alterations, and we also have rooms for storage of the vintage period stock we use primarily for extras. There are generally three or four teams of fitters constantly at work on each upcoming episode in addition to the staff who sort and catalog the clothes as they are fit. With over nine thousand extras in season three alone, dauntingly massive quantities of incoming and outgoing pieces of clothing need to be tracked with machine-like precision, so an utter state of frenzy often reigns!

"That's what happens when you let someone have an entire room for skirts." —*ABE*

PINNINGS & UNDERPINNINGS

"It's the bras. And the girdles. And the corsets, all designed to cut off the circulation to your brain, so you walk around on the verge of passing out . . ." —MIDGE

Bras, girdles, corsets, slips, petticoats, garters . . . ! The underpinnings of '50s fashion provide the structural frames on which the period's architectural shapes were built. And having designed a great many—especially eighteenth-century—period costumes, I welcomed the opportunity to immerse myself in the equally stylized, equally glamorous silhouettes of the 1950s, one of the last periods in which understructures played such a critical role in creating the shapes of women's clothing.

With my team I began collecting as many original pieces as possible, but since we couldn't rely on vintage stock alone to provide for the myriad body types in the cast, we expanded our stock with facsimiles made to order by contemporary manufacturers. It was the *only* way to get the vintage clothing to fit correctly and look right on hundreds of extras. So every woman who appears on camera was first dressed in appropriate lingerie, beginning with girdles and bras of every type—bullet, strapless, longline—the shapes of which we then refined by hand with foam and falsies.

"In a girdle you can't feel a damn thing." —MIDGE

But our principal characters, Midge in particular, posed more specific challenges, not only in terms of silhouette

26

but comfort, and after trying many vintage bras on Midge, we found only two that worked at all—and in fact only one that worked perfectly! It therefore became a precious object gingerly nursed through season one, and it was only during prep for season two, after numerous unsuccessful attempts, that we finally found a builder in France who was able to copy it flawlessly. Humbled, I realized I'd never fully appreciated the level of skill and artistry involved in creating '50s lingerie!

Midge's other essential understructure, then, was a version of a corset used primarily for body shaping in haute couture. Also custom-made, it was designed to be more flexible, and therefore less confining and uncomfortable, than a classic '50s girdle since she would be in it for many hours every day.

And then there were the airier understructures—the many fluffy petticoats that filled the racks of our studio like pastel clouds, the final underlayers in a fundamentally layered approach to dressing. The fullness of each petticoat varied depending on the shape of the skirt or skirts with which it was meant to be worn, and we'd experiment with multiple combinations and variations. Then, in order to track which petticoat options worked with each specific garment, they were labeled and arranged on racks alphabetically. So while Midge's wedding dress might be worn with petticoats A, C, and/ or D, her yellow Catskills dress might require petticoats B and/or E. And so, on many early mornings, alphabet madness prevailed!

EXQUISITE SKELETONS

In some cases, a garment's understructure is completely inseparable from it—like a skeleton. Innovative fashion designers from this period like Dior, Givenchy, Charles James, and others often designed from the inside out to create intriguing sculptural forms that seemed to defy gravity, and I adopted this approach for Midge's strapless USO performance dress with its built-in corset. This type of integrated understructure, meant to create the appearance of being worn without support, was fairly typical of '50s couture, which was often about illusion, and with that type of garment the skeleton inside can be as fascinating and beautiful as its casing.

ALL THE TRIMMINGS

"Everything with Midge starts with an accessory." —ROSE

Rose's comment echoes one of my pet mantras for Midge and for the series overall. The countless beautiful, elegant designs of the late 1950s were characteristically supplemented with hats, shoes, gloves, handbags, and jewelry, which, though they were meant to be comparably stylish, could also at times be unpredictably whimsical. And that element of sheer whimsy played a great part for me in designing the accessories for the show, with, every now and then, a particularly fanciful hat or handbag becoming the basis for a whole look.

We collected and used a number of original vintage pieces, especially handbags, shoes, and jewelry, but designed and built the greater part of the hats and gloves for the principals, as well as some of Midge's shoes. Without question, the hats were the most demanding items to produce, and beyond being merely decorative, without them many costumes were incomplete.

The overwhelming variety that exists in hats from this period is a testament to the expressive ingenuity of the madly marvelous milliners who made them, and to their often poetic, wildly fantastical creativity. Without a simple how-to guide, I found myself journeying down a different creative path each time an outfit needed a *crowning* touch. And while I started off studying actual hats in books and period magazines, I quickly progressed to exotic land and sea animals and plants for inspiration.

Every hat for Midge or Rose, played by Marin Hinkle, became a mini sculpture—starting with an approximate form, finding the material that could be sculpted to create and maintain that form, then fitting the actor. And upon completion, the hats became signature elements of each look. Rachel once told me that she only really felt her character, Midge, emerge when her hat was placed on her head. So on days when her costume called for a hat, in what became a practiced little ritual before shooting, Rachel, the hair designer, and I would position it with ceremony before she set off for set. And sometimes we'd discover, in that final suspenseful moment, that it needed an additional tweak or a tilt to the right or left, and even once, to our surprise—for the divorce court scene in season three—we ended up turning the hat entirely around!

Many of the hats for both Midge and Rose were made from colored felts, despite the difficulty of finding distinctive colors and textures, since so many long-established European felt houses have closed. For inspiration, we'd often arrange the felts we found on a table in the studio to create a chromatic display, where, when the story moved to summer settings like the Catskills or Miami, the felts were superseded by straws and other lightweight materials. The straws, even more difficult to find than the felts, were more delicate and translucent, but also more amenable to surface treatment, so we'd often add decorative elements to enhance their originality—or even eccentricity—like for Midge's hat in the Catskills boating scene daubed with petals and butterflies, her Fontainebleau arrival hat flecked with gauzy, pastel silk flowers, or her beach hat in Miami spun with spiraling, geometric forms.

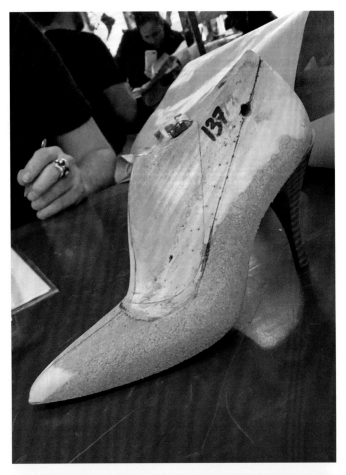

"I get it now, why men rule the world: no high heels." —MIDGE

Shoes and handbags had to be sourced extensively, especially shoes, and women's shoes were especially hard to find in good condition. And to complement the hats and bags that accompanied nearly every outfit, especially for Midge, we also needed pairs upon pairs of gloves—gloves that would be versatile enough to work both in an exterior scene with a coat and handbag, or in an interior with a silk dress. The weight of the leather was therefore crucial, so after extensive swatching we concluded that very soft suedes were the best material for the luxurious, sensual quality we wanted. And due to the specificity of the colors I was working with, the dearth of extant period gloves in wearable condition, and the lack of surviving glovers in America, we ended up having them made in England and Italy.

MIDGE

PURSES

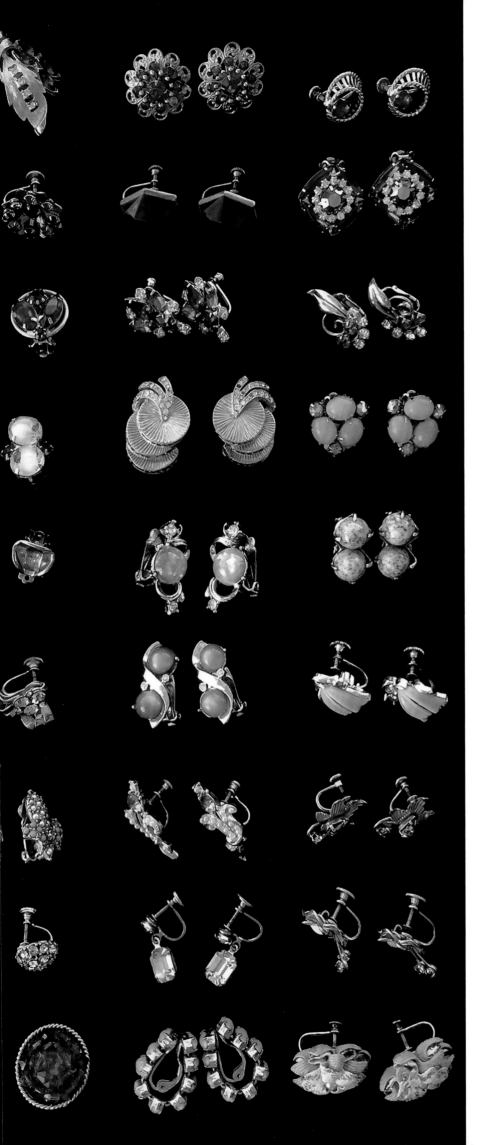

*"If women don't
realize what's going
on in the world, they
won't step in and fix it.
Because they will fix
it. And accessorize it!"*
—MIDGE

In addition to men's ties,
and hats for both men and
women, probably the most
enjoyable type of accessory
to collect was the women's
jewelry. Sometimes the
smallest items can have the
biggest impact, and once
again, it seemed like we
could never have enough.
And since we put jewelry
on every extra and prin-
cipal individually every
morning, to transport the
many pieces of jewelry to
set we built little wooden
carts on wheels with black
velvet-padded drawers, like
carts of colored candy.

Choosing Midge's jewelry
was another daily ritual.
Usually a pair of earrings,
a watch, and sometimes
a necklace completed her
look, and I would prepare a
tray with her best options
every morning. These, then,
were the last few precious
moments in which to com-
mune over the character
in a specific scene, and the
final step in establishing
the costume before it was
captured forever on camera.

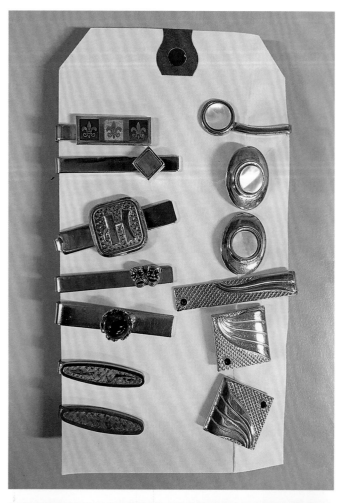

*"Bald men can be attractive—
with the right hat."* —MIDGE

Extensive, ongoing searches were equally critical to developing our men's wardrobe. It seemed like we could never have enough ties! And for extras' ties, we created racks of color-coded hangers so the fitters could quickly find a tie or selection of ties to coordinate with a costume's overall palette. A tie is often the most telling element of a man's costume, and the shape was already changing from 1958 to 1959—not yet '60s skinny but no longer as wide as the earlier part of the decade—so I also felt it was really important to use this transitional width as much as possible.

Men's hats were also experiencing a moment of transition. The brims were not as wide as earlier hats, but still not quite as narrow as the early 1960s, though the lighter-weight straw hats we used in Las Vegas and Miami had brims that were *slightly* narrower, just starting to close the gap with the later period.

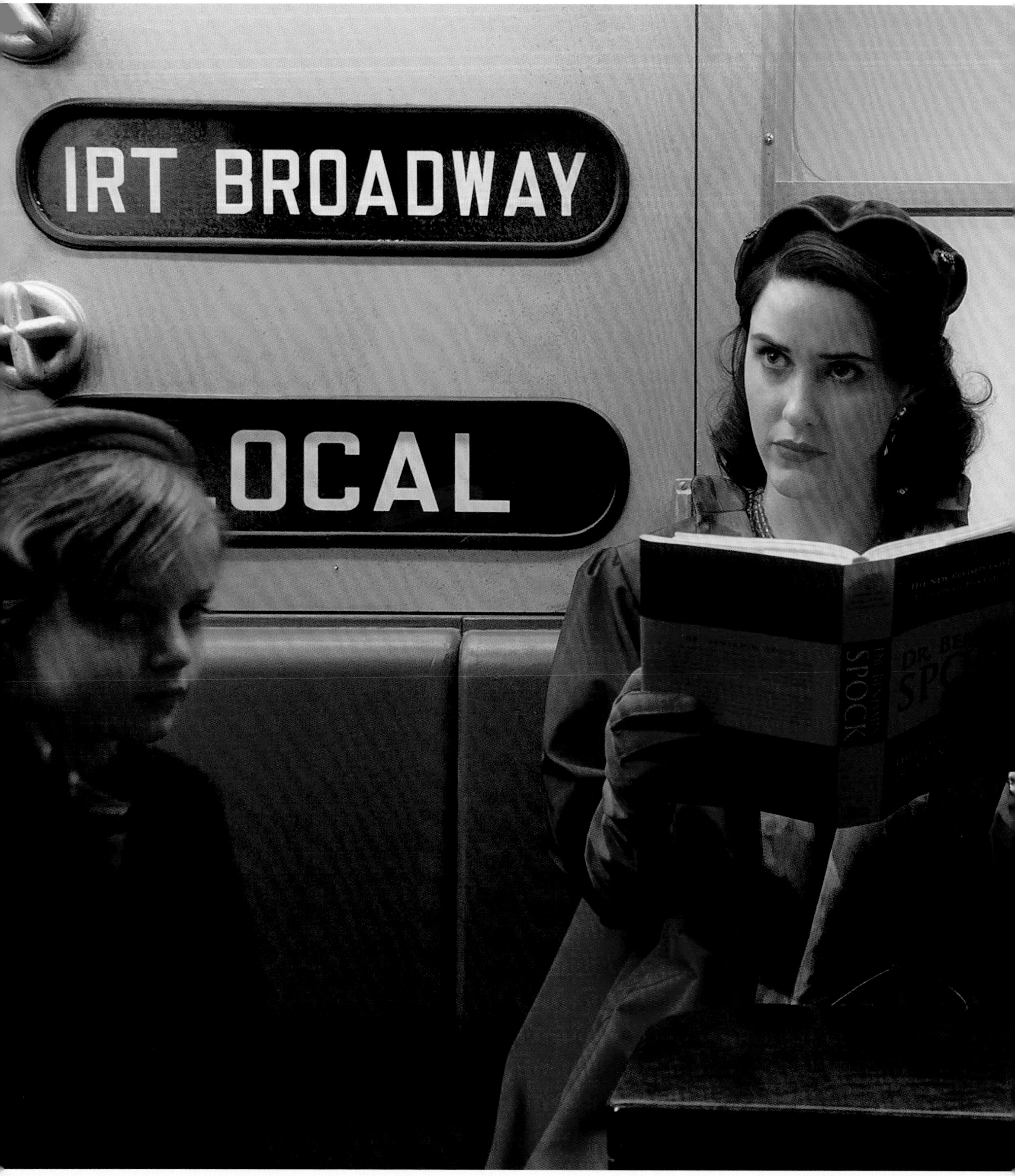
IRT BROADWAY
OCAL
SPOCK

Uptown / Downtown

The Color Pink

"My favorite color's pink."
—MIDGE

It all began with a pink coat and well over two hundred—pink, of course!—swatches . . .

After perusing the pilot script and being introduced to the then still nascent character, Miriam, aka "Midge," Maisel née Weissman, by her creator, Amy Sherman-Palladino, and fellow writer and director Daniel Palladino, I remember being particularly taken by Amy's capsule description of Midge as "a character who *never* seems depressed."

. . . And I started to think . . . pink!

For though I might not normally have chosen to link the color pink with such an irrepressibly indomitable character, I began to imagine that for Midge, who seemingly so ingenuously sees the world and her life through rose-colored glasses at the beginning of the series, "seeing pink" could also eventually come to express the triumphant part of her nature by, in fact, becoming her defense against dejection and defeat. So the upheaval in her married life, rather than triggering a denial or rejection of the pink in her past, could and would result in an affirmative transformation, like a magical transmutation, of the very *meaning* of pink.

PANTONE®
694 C

PANTONE®
493 C

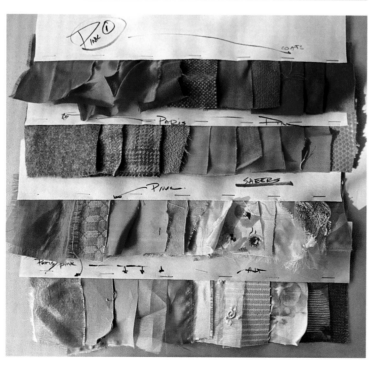

The Marvelous Mrs. Maisel

CHARACTER: 1. MIDGE

ACTOR: RACHEL BROSNAHAN

SWATCH	SWATCH	SWATCH
		MAD
DYE/PAINT		
SOURCE/YARDAGE/S		
COSTUME ITEM	COSTUME ITEM	COSTUME ITEM
BUTCHER SHOP COAT	BUTCHER SHOP COAT LINING	BUTCHER SHOP DRESS

MIDGE (2)
pink silk
dress - NYE

IN THE PINK

I felt that Midge first needed to be seen in what would then become her emblematic color. So pink, in the first episode, would be both a badge of identity and a source of strength, and then, in sometimes conspicuous, sometime subtle ways, continue to resurface in her wardrobe throughout the series. It surprised me just how much we all grew attached to it, and it ultimately became the signature color of the show.

In the pilot, the garment most inseparably bound to her identity is the pink swing coat she wears in the first musical montage after the wedding, the first of many coats—of many colors!—that I started to refer to as her multicolored armor. It's our first impression of married Midge (four years on), and since it's a defining look of the pilot, I wanted the coat's color to send the right message—feminine, but not *too* feminine; sweet, but not *too* sweet— a color that's seductive to watch whether Midge is breezing sunnily through the Upper West Side, or drenched with rain before her first extempore performance at the Gaslight.

Then, after amassing more than two hundred swatches of available fabric in search of the perfect pink for her coat, I realized we were never just going to chance upon the *quintessential* pink. Our sole recourse was to brew it ourselves in vast, rosy vats of dye—a solution we'd then resort to with regularity.

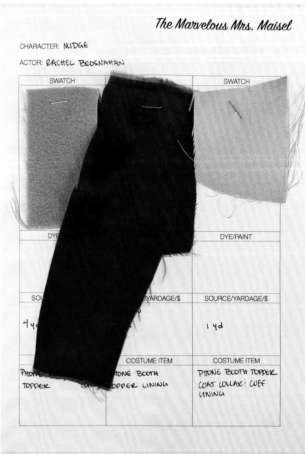

The Marvelous Mrs. Maisel

CHARACTER: MIDGE

ACTOR: RACHEL BROSNAHAN

SWATCH		SWATCH
DYE		DYE/PAINT
SOU	YARDAGE/$	SOURCE/YARDAGE/$
4 yd		1 yd
	COSTUME ITEM	COSTUME ITEM
PHONE TOPPER	TONE BOOTH OPPER LINING	PHONE BOOTH TOPPER COAT COLLAR: CUFF LINING

The Marvelous Mrs. Maisel

CHARACTER: MIDGE MAISEL

ACTOR: RACHEL BROSNAHAN

SWATCH	SWATCH	SWATCH
DYE/PAINT	DYE/PAINT	DYE/PAINT
SOURCE/YARDAGE/$	SOURCE/YARDAGE/$	SOURCE/YARDAGE/$
SILK WOOL BALLERINA	2 yds 55"	2 yds
COSTUME ITEM	COSTUME ITEM	COSTUME ITEM
DRESS	COLLAR	LINING

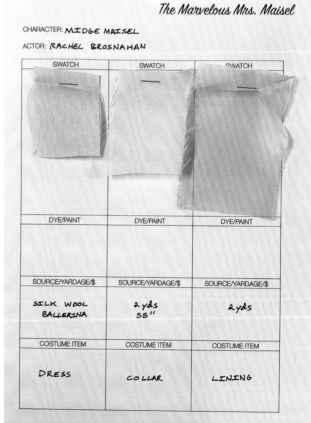

49

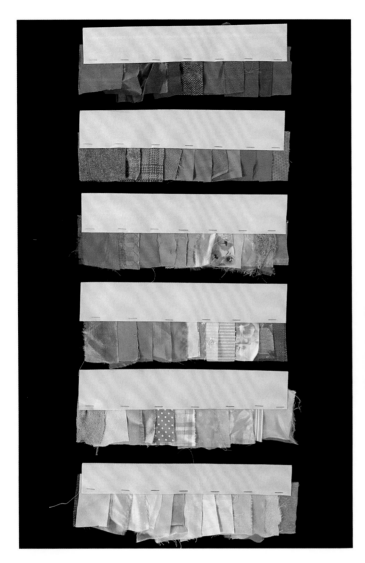

A PINK FOR
ALL SEASONS

As the series progressed, I reintroduced the color pink in a multitude of different shades, intending for it to become a color with history and memory, a color that viewers could either recognize consciously or might respond to intuitively—an echo, as it were, that reconnects Midge to her past and gives her character strength and continuity.

Sometimes very subtly so. . . . On her first day of work at B. Altman, her collar and cuffs are trimmed—*very* discreetly—with bits of pink ribbon. And for her appearance in divorce court in season three, she wears a deep

pink fabric *under* her collar—in both cases, perhaps, for self-confidence. In fact, *whenever* she wears the color pink, whether as an element of clothing or an accessory or a trim, it's meant to reaffirm her unswerving tenacity.

There was often a bit of madness in our discussions and explorations of the color pink, and I started to imagine that, like a mist, the color seeped into and through the costumes even when it wasn't used overtly. And though other colors also grew in significance as her story progressed, the trajectory of the color pink—as raspberry, fuchsia, peach, coral, salmon, cherry, orchid, or even bubblegum!—is the longest and most resonant, the one that remains inseparable from Midge's marvelous journey.

51

CHAPTER 02

Coats of Many Colors

"Get your coat."

—SUSIE

A coat is often the most dramatic element in a wardrobe. And it can often be a character's most defining piece of clothing, since it dominates their overall silhouette and determines how they're first perceived in relation to other characters. But I can't even begin to express how, more than any other element of clothing, the coat became the *most* conspicuous part of Midge's wardrobe, as her rainbow closet of coats became inseparable from her persona.

The prototype, the pink coat in the pilot that incited the Midge coat mania, was a version of a classic '50s swing coat, fitted on top and full at the bottom—like a bell, a shape that lends itself naturally to, well, swinging! And in scenes where Midge is on the move—like skipping and twirling up Riverside Drive—as her flapping, fluttering, flying coats seem to sweep her along, I started to consider the coat her equivalent of a superhero cape—the transfiguring, protective, emotional armor that emboldens and empowers her as a character.

SOMEWHERE OVER THE RAINBOW

Then, just as the pinkness of the first coat echoed Midge's rosy outlook at the beginning of the series, each coat of an*other* color ended up mirroring yet another aspect of her expanding emotional landscape. The spectrum of colors I used for her coats grew in direct proportion to her character, with each new shade reinforcing the expression of a distinctive—and distinctively Midge—state of mind.

I began to think of *green* coats as being worn in scenes of heroic independence, like her impromptu rally speech in Washington Square Park, and *white* coats during scenes of cathartic closure or renewal, like "All Alone," the moving finale sequence of season two. She wears an *orange*

coat with a warm, comic feeling to the Stage Deli for her rendezvous with comedy hack Herb Smith, played by Wallace Shawn. And certain coats were designed to be very situation-specific, like the *magenta* Jacques Fath coat she borrows from Rose for her first appearance in court, with its details much more typical of glamorous '50s evening wear—the kind of coat she'd wear when she needed an extra dose of courage.

Since each new coat was destined to accompany a new, uncharted phase of Midge's journey, designing a closetful of coats, with their many variations in shape and color, became almost an obsession for me. I took it as a personal challenge to conjure up each "next one," and several racks of Midge's coats soon occupied a dominant place in my office. I sometimes felt I was lost myself in a forest of coats—of many colors!—trying to find my way . . .

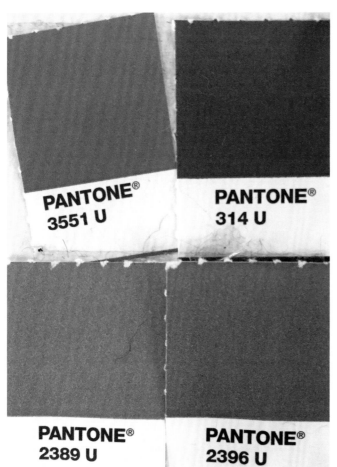

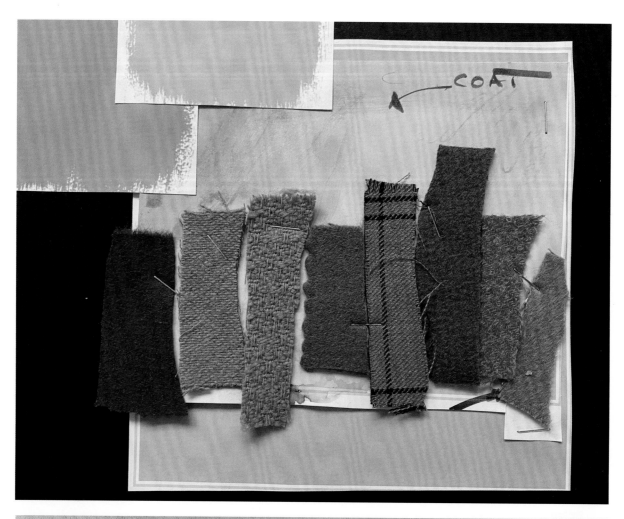

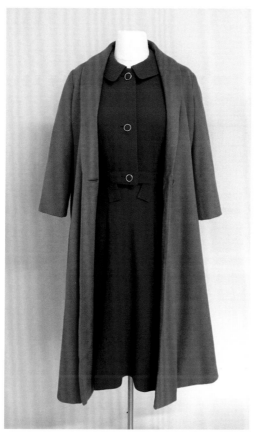

SUGAR-COATING!

Since for so many people, the coats really seemed to encapsulate the magic of Mrs. Maisel, they were singled out often to represent both the character and the show. And by the third season, their persistent appeal led to my designing a small collection of Midge-inspired coats for a charity auction at Bergdorf Goodman—which is now, of course, my favorite store on Fifth Avenue!

And the original pink coat from the pilot now lives at the Smithsonian Institution, in the archives of the National Museum of American History—fittingly, with Dorothy's ruby slippers and Superman's cape!

CHAPTER 03

Like a Dream

"Perfect wedding, perfect breakfast, perfect life."
—MIDGE

Glimpses of Midge's would-be, picture-perfect past—before, during, and after her wedding and prior to breaking up with her husband Joel—recur throughout the series as a reminder of the contrast between her naively idealistic expectations and the insecure but exhilarating life she leads thereafter. And because we view the rose-colored past primarily through Midge's eyes, I mainly tried to focus on designing looks that were sure to have a pivotal place in her memory.

. . . And then, of course, color them Midge!

For while a clothing-conscious character like Midge would have an acute recollection of what everyone was wearing, she might also project a sense of what could or *should* have been worn in any given scene. So the costumes had to be relevant both to the past and present stories, and provide not only exposition but insight into Midge's own ideas about her past and present selves.

PAST PERFECT

"It's like a dream . . . " —MIDGE

In effect, the wedding is the overture of season one, and the first massive scene I had to costume. The guests at the reception were all subject to a very specific palette, with the bridesmaids' dresses built from multiple layers of green organza, the other women dressed in creamy whites and seafoam greens and blues, and the wedding band in salmon pink tuxedos, all to create a poetic impression of Midge as a cloud floating freely over a sea of pale, delicate tones.

"White is a very tricky color." —MIDGE

The centerpiece, of course, was Midge's wedding dress, which I wanted to be exquisitely feminine, but more minimalist in approach than classic 1950s "layer-cake" gowns with their tiers of lace, beads, and trim. Ultimately, the simple, graceful Givenchy wedding dress worn by Audrey Hepburn in *Funny Face* was a major inspiration, and I tried to retain the airy, ethereal feeling of the original while adapting the basic cut of the dress to Midge.

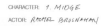

The Marvelous Mrs. Maisel

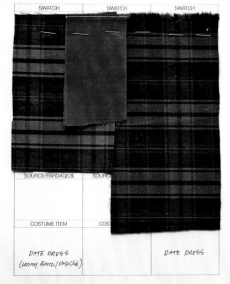

CHARACTER: 1. MIDGE
ACTOR: RACHEL BROSNAHAN

DREAMS WITHIN A DREAM

For the flashbacks that intersperse her wedding mono-
logue, which evoke an even earlier time in her past—her
college days at Bryn Mawr and her first romantic encounters with Joel, played by Michael Zegen—the colors I used
were closer to primary colors, with a heavy dose of playful patterns and plaids, and with fuller skirts and more
petticoats to achieve an earlier '50s silhouette. The plaid
dress I made for the date on which Joel introduces Midge
to stand-up comedy in the person of Lenny Bruce, played
by Luke Kirby, was based on an early Claire McCardell,
and I used that shape again, in pink, for the moving-in
scene in a later flashback sequence (episode 104), hoping
to make the most of its full silhouette and asymmetrical
bodice to capture the earlier period.

As at the other Seven Sisters schools, Bryn Mawr stu-
dents typically wore a combination of plaid skirts, neatly
shaped, colored sweaters, and primly cute blouses
beneath the essential Bryn Mawr uniform blazer. In
Midge's case, I put her into a rosy sweater to keep her in
tones that were still seductively wistful. But the uniform
blazer itself presented something of a challenge, since
there were numerous girls to costume on a tight deadline.
Ultimately, then, I found a school uniform manufacturer
in England who still built a jacket close in shape to the
ones I was seeing in photos from the period, which we
ordered "as is" in various sizes, then adapted by recon-
structing the shoulders and adding the Bryn Mawr
logo—individually embroidered!—to each breast pocket.

The Marvelous Mrs. Maisel

CHARACTER: MIDGE

ACTOR: RACHEL BROSNAHAN

		SWATCH
		DYE/PAINT
SOURCE/YARDAGE/$	SOURCE/YARDAGE/$	SOURCE/YARDAGE/$
STOCK	2YRDS	
COSTUME ITEM	COSTUME ITEM	COSTUME ITEM
S3-19 #5A DINER FLASHBACK LOOK SKIRT 308	S3-19 #5B WOOL JERSEY TOP DINER FLASHBACK	

66

HAPPY DAYS ARE(N'T) HERE AGAIN

In a later flashback montage (episode 104), set to Barbra Streisand's rendition of "Happy Days Are Here Again," we collaged a few of the classically happier moments in Midge's life between her wedding and separation from Joel—being carried over the threshold of their first apartment, eating Chinese food on the floor by candlelight, moving in, bringing their first baby home, and other brief interludes representing '50s marital bliss.

I decided to call the pale blue suit Midge wears when carried into their empty apartment her "Marie

Antoinette look"—the image of a young princess making an entrance into her palace—with a collar of small sea pearls and a little crown-like fascinator, a piece that actually once belonged to my mother and was part of her vast collection.

Then, when Midge recrosses the threshold carrying her first baby, we see her in a pregnancy smock that mixes lavender, pink, and baby blue, a look meant to render Midge the personification of motherhood, and for the remainder of the montage she continues to radiate contentment in her role as the consummate young mother and wife.

GREEN ON GREEN

But once again, the real purpose of the costumes in these fragments is to emphasize the contrast between her nostalgia for an idealized past and the divergent path that her life then takes in the series, which the green-to-green-dress flashback that concludes the "Happy Days" montage portrays in a poignant way.

In that finale, there are two contrasting but complementary dresses of almost identical forest green, one for the last flashback to a New Year's party past, the other for the melancholic moment in which Midge is moving out of her apartment after her marriage has collapsed. As the song ends, an upbeat silk party dress with a flouncy, full-shaped silhouette, emblematic of Midge's previous happy days with Joel, morphs seamlessly into a narrow, formfitting wool-crêpe sheath with a more mature, sober feeling. The transition was accomplished with a complicated camera dissolve from identical positions on the backs of the two green dresses, so although the dresses were different in shape and texture, their backs were designed to match perfectly in the dissolve, as Midge's spirit flows from idyllic past to imperfect present, from dream to reality.

CHAPTER 04

Exercise in Color: Dressing *Up*(town)

*"Where'd you learn that, on the
mean streets of the Upper West Side?"*
—SUSIE

In many ways the uptown scenes were extensions into the present tense of the rose-colored world of the flashbacks, the idealized world—and lifestyle—so ardently cherished by Midge at the beginning of the series. A bubble of postwar, upper middle-class affluence and optimism, in which both Midge and Rose ostensibly emulate the conventional 1950s role of women as professional wives, homemakers, and mothers. Living the dream meant living the myth—in a surface world of artificial happiness, a world of conformity and order, the world of the Upper West Side.

Dressing uptown meant dressing *up*. Clothing was coded and decorous, and though I filled the uptown scenes with color, the palette was primarily muted and pale with a strong emphasis on pastels. Elegant but comfortable, cozy, reassuring colors meant to reinforce a general aura of pleasing complacency. Accessories, like tempting baubles, were often the most colorful parts of an outfit, and I used them to add accents to the costume of every extra. I set up boards of color inspiration for the fitters, so that, in our idealized uptown world, a woman in, say, a lavender suit would be sure to have a *perfectly* complementary olive-toned bag and shoes, and finish off her look with an *amazingly* coordinated hat to tie it together.

Color became an important story element with substantial narrative impact in *Mrs. Maisel,* and it began on the "mean streets of the Upper West Side," to quote Susie from season three—in the butcher shop, the exercise classes, the walks in the park, the synagogue. . . . For, despite the seductively pleasing ambient palette of the Weissmans' world, it was ephemeral, fragile, illusory, and easily shattered or damaged. The balance—or fluctuation—between this artificially perfect world and the conflicting events that followed was the real Midge Maisel drama for me, and as the story unfolded, I often found I was using color as if I were scoring a musical, with corresponding emotional highs and lows. So, as the Maisel world exploded with color, I even started dubbing certain colors "echo tones" because they recurred like leitmotifs to evoke past moments or feelings.

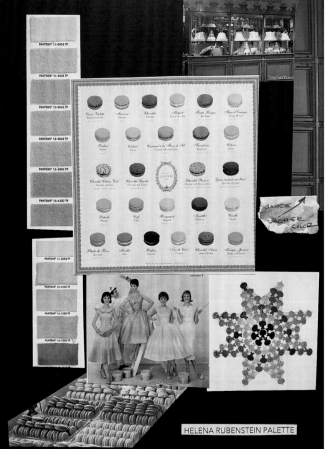

HELENA RUBENSTEIN PALETTE

"Rag doll down!" —CLAIRE

The exercise class, with its pastel colors and playful, girlish spirit, most clearly epitomized the Upper West Side palette. In fact, the colors were shamelessly (!) inspired by the many-colored macarons from the tearoom Ladurée that were one of my own guilty pleasures when I was studying painting in Paris. Then, in the course of my research, I discovered some images of Helena Rubinstein's "Beauty School" in black and white, with women gripping bottles between their feet as exercise gear. And I was instantly enthralled by the idea of designing a roomful of women in pastry pastels performing period body work!

"Is this how you look in the morning?"
—BENJAMIN

Even at home, Midge's wardrobe continues to reflect her lively relationship with color. In her pastel nightwear, she wafts through both apartments like a cotton-candy-colored cloud, since classic '50s nightgowns were often lacy, sheer, and unmistakably romantic. They were among the few real vintage pieces we actually used on Midge, the notable exception being the pale blue nightgown she wore to the Gaslight in episode 101, which had to be rigged to be pulled off and on very quickly.

I also reserved a special capri look for Midge at home, to meet her occasional need to retreat from her newfound role as a brash comic to being just a child or daughter again. So we see her in pink capris just after she moves back in with her parents, then in deep blue with a gray-toned top when she and Rose are planning her wedding with Benjamin.

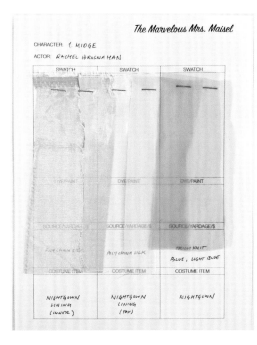

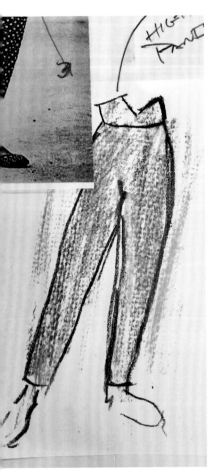

The Marvelous Mrs. Maisel

CHARACTER: MIDGE

ACTOR: Rachel Brosnahan

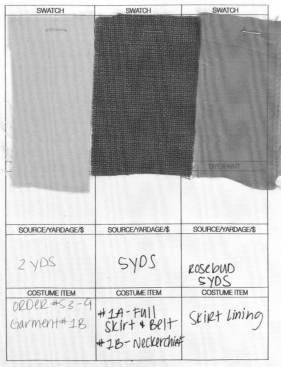

SWATCH	SWATCH	SWATCH
SOURCE/YARDAGE/$	SOURCE/YARDAGE/$	SOURCE/YARDAGE/$
2 YDS	5 YDS	ROSEBUD 5 YDS
COSTUME ITEM	COSTUME ITEM	COSTUME ITEM
ORDER #53-9 Garment #1B	#1A-Full skirt & belt #1B-Neckerchief	Skirt Lining

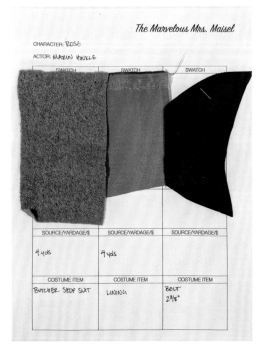

"No one uses Rose's pink soap."
—IMOGENE

But Rose is the ultimate archetype of the uptown aesthetic—as well as the progenitor of Midge's obsession with pink. Our series creator Amy told me she conceived of Rose as a woman who aspired to a touch of Hollywood glamour in her life, so I designed a series of elegant robes and dressing gowns that indulged her desire for mystery, aloofness, and allure. I worked with Indian and Japanese silk brocades, focusing mainly on lighter tones in season one and moving into deeper, more vibrant colors by season three. And the robes proved key in helping Rose to theatricalize her distress in various moments of adversity, starting with the collapse of Midge's marriage.

In fact, at the beginning of the series, we are led to believe that Midge is quite decisively on the path to becoming another Rose. She has an apartment in the same building that mirrors her mother's, and she regularly raids her mother's wardrobe. She inherits her instinct for fashion and color from Rose, and Rose is clearly her role model, mentor, and guru in the Way of All Things Pink. In fact, the Weissmans' Morningside Drive apartment is Midge's pink sanctuary, often filled with blushing pink flower arrangements, where even the cook and housekeeper Zelda, played by Matilda Szydagis, is uniformed in pink!

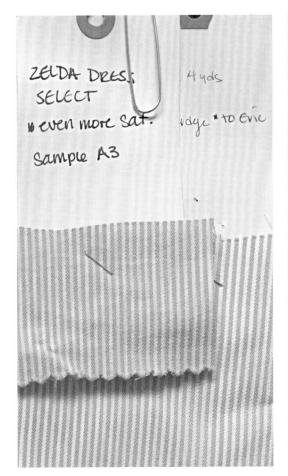

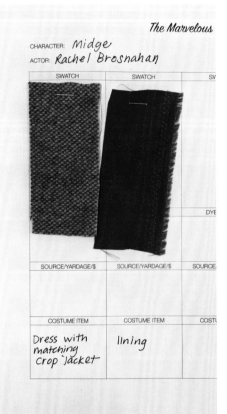

The Marvelous

CHARACTER: *Midge*
ACTOR: *Rachel Brosnahan*

SWATCH	SWATCH	SW
		DYE
SOURCE/YARDAGE/$	SOURCE/YARDAGE/$	SOURCE
COSTUME ITEM	COSTUME ITEM	COSTU
Dress with matching Crop Jacket	lining	

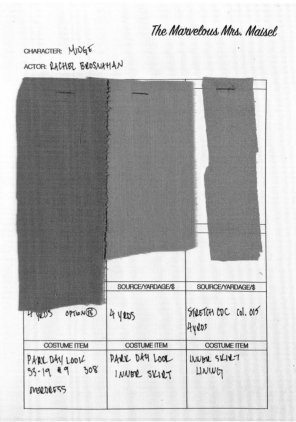

The Marvelous Mrs. Maisel

CHARACTER: MIDGE

ACTOR: RACHEL BROSNAHAN

	SOURCE/YARDAGE/$	SOURCE/YARDAGE/$
4 YRDS OPTION B	4 YRDS	STRETCH CDC COL. 015 4 YRDS
COSTUME ITEM	COSTUME ITEM	COSTUME ITEM
PARK DAY LOOK SS-19 #9 308 SHIRTDRESS	PARK DAY LOOK INNER SKIRT	INNER SKIRT LINING

CHAPTER 05

Color by Gaslight: Dressing *Down*(town)

*"It's downtown. If you have
underwear on, you're overdressed."*
—MIDGE

In the late '50s, there were significant social and cultural divides between the various neighborhoods of Manhattan, epitomized in the series by the gulf between the worlds of uptown and downtown, the staid bourgeois and unruly, rebellious bohemian.

In Greenwich Village, the heart of the more ethnically diverse, arty, radical New York subculture, painters, sculptors, poets, and musicians intermingled with working-class families, often first-generation Italian immigrants. Inspired by Parisian bohemian culture, clothing styles were simpler but symbolically charged, driven by a deliberate anti-aesthetic that extolled an ideal of dressing *down*. In the self-conscious attempt to display a pose of indifference to fashion, work clothes, sweaters, and sweatshirts were rampant. And the palette was generally darker and earthier, paired with the archetypal "beatnik" penchant for black—capris, jeans, leotards, turtlenecks!—a color or *non*-color that was basically taboo in upper middle-class circles apart from formal wear.

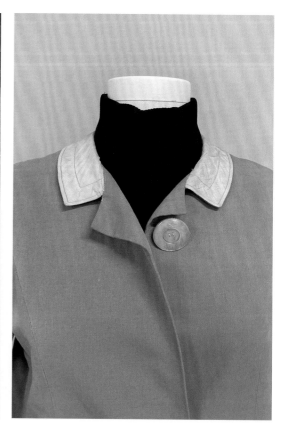

"We can just . . . go downtown and be cool cats by night." —MIDGE

Midge makes a major effort to develop a downtown image to complement Joel's clumsy attempts to cultivate an after-hours, "cool cat" look for his stand-up spots at the Gaslight. With her own natural aptitude as a social chameleon, Midge's look was subdued and somber enough to jibe with the downtown palette, veering towards beatnik black, but with as many alternate, richly dark tones as possible, varying blacks with deep burgundies, bottle greens, and rich aubergines.

And so, very *dark* capris, boleros, turtlenecks, and fitted wool stretch tops snuck into her more characteristically bright, exuberant wardrobe. Structured hats were exchanged for sheer headscarves, and her absolute must-wear heels replaced by flats that resembled ballet slippers. Even her buff-colored raincoat had an earthy informality that reinforced her downtown image, with only a passing resemblance to the Midge of the Upper West Side.

"The one who looks like she lives under a bridge." —*MIDGE*

The supreme representative of the downtown world for Midge was her new fan, ally, sidekick, friend, and eventual manager, Susie, played by Alex Borstein. With a basically androgynous feeling and a somewhat comic undertone, Susie's clothing was designed to make her feel safe and look tough. And since it was clear from the start that she wouldn't have much variation in her wardrobe, every element had to be spot on.

The motorcycle jacket was our starting point, and she wore it like a turtle's protective shell. At first we used a vintage jacket, but by the end of season one, the leather had so completely dried out that Alex could hardly move, so we then copied the original, detail by detail, in a more forgiving leather. Her signature trousers were also reproduced in various fabrics from a pair of Swedish army pants we initially liked because we felt they gave Susie a slightly—anachronistically!—hip-hop vibe.

Then there were the nearly-impossible-to-find-but-had-to-be-perfect engineering boots, the necklace of keys, the striped sweaters, and the indispensable cap. The boots, in the end, were a pair of my own I'd once purchased in Vienna while designing a theater piece there. The keys that Susie wears around her neck—so as never to lose them!—are, of course, the keys to the Gaslight, and Alex wanted to use them as her only piece of jewelry, which of course was perfect for the character.

The sweaters? After finding two vintage sweaters that were ideal but riddled with moth holes, I decided to have some new ones knit at a shop that still had a machine old enough to be able to reproduce the small period stitch.

And the hat! . . . In the first two seasons she wore a classic European fisherman's cap that I'd aged to look worn. Then, for season three, as Susie in her new managerial mindset gets progressively more conscious of her own image, I found an unusual mariner's cap, with, I thought, an even more perfect shape to accompany Susie's evolution—from fisherman to skipper?—and built her a new one.

90

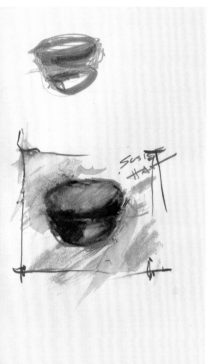

*"A nice clean-cut young man,
someone your mother would love."*
—*JACKIE*

As an aspiring comic himself in season
one, Joel is in fact the instigator of Midge's
downtown adventures, and his own look
alternates between Midtown business
conservative and would-be Village hip.
We built all of his suits for season one in
a subtle, cool palette of light blues and
grays. So, while the choice of an iconic
black turtleneck sweater is for him a no
doubt radical choice and testifies to the
extent of his desire to be welcomed into
the downtown scene, it hardly offsets the
persistence of his basically clean, conservative '50s look.

"We could be downtown people," he
ventures, tentatively, to Midge. But then,
when his black turtleneck is mysteriously
attacked by moths, it seems an ominous
portent of the unraveling of his marriage
and his career. And of course, we had
multiple sweaters prepped and ready for
the scene with precisely identical holes—
thanks to our scrupulous, in-house
wardrobe moths!

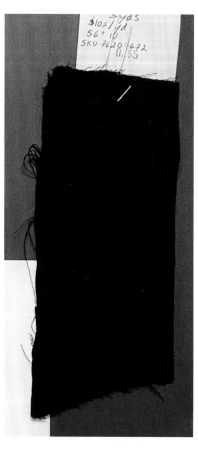

CHARACTER: Midge
ACTOR: Rachel Brosnahan

SWATCH   SWATCH

DYE/PAINT

SOURCE/YARDAGE/$ SOURCE/YARDAG

COSTUME ITEM   COSTUME ITE

Coat   Coat linin

94

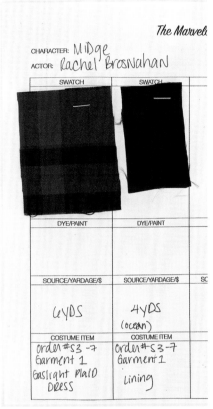

The Marvelo

CHARACTER: MIDGE
ACTOR: Rachel Brosnahan

"That dress needs pearls." —ROSE

For Midge's official coming out as the stand-up "Mrs. Maisel," introduced by Lenny Bruce at the Gaslight in episode 108, we created the black dress that became the prototype for Midge's many subsequent performance looks. From the very first days of the show, Amy had a black dress and pearls in mind for this moment. And the specific dress was inspired by the simple black cocktail dress with bows at the shoulders worn by Audrey Hepburn in *Sabrina* for her first "date" with Humphrey Bogart. For Midge's date—with destiny!—I found an *especially* beautiful Italian silk that had an alluring luster under lights, and the resulting dress became the first of her many Mrs. Maisel "limelight looks," as we eventually called her performance costumes.

This was the real beginning of her new life and career, and there would be no turning back.

CHAPTER 06

Up, Down, All Around

"Oh, I don't have a persona. I'm just me."
—MIDGE

Even when she's a spectator or a tourist, Midge can always be counted on to dress for the occasion—and the place! But as her story evolves, the distinctions between her up- and downtown looks become less rigid. She starts to display a more fluid, all-around style as she shuttles more comfortably back and forth—or up and down!—between what were initially two neatly contrasting worlds.

In Washington Square, the nucleus of downtown bohemian culture, her basically uptown look had a relaxed, dressed-down quality that allowed her to feel that she could fit in both uptown and down. And then, at Jane Jacobs' rally, where she also discovers another sense of what a performer can be—political!—her outfit becomes yet another impromptu performance look, reinforcing her growing conviction that she can be both herself and still, either spontaneously or intuitively, perfectly dressed for the microphone.

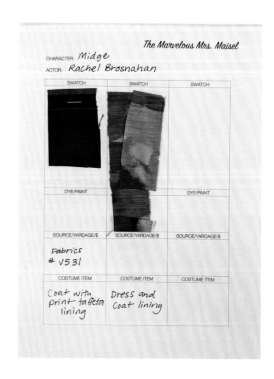

The Marvelous Mrs. Maisel
CHARACTER: Midge
ACTOR: Rachel Brosnahan

SWATCH	SWATCH	SWATCH
DYE/PAINT		DYE/PAINT
SOURCE/YARDAGE/$	SOURCE/YARDAGE/$	SOURCE/YARDAGE/$
Fabrics # V531		
COSTUME ITEM	COSTUME ITEM	COSTUME ITEM
Coat with print taffeta lining	Dress and Coat lining	

"What's with the duds?"
—**KESSLER**

And as she tries out different performance looks in search of an original stage identity, Midge responds more and more readily to the theatrical in her life and looks *off*-stage. The *overly* elegant coat and dress she wears to meet her lawyer Kessler, played by Max Casella, and then, at his suggestion, to court, is a choice example. I call it her "Jacques Fath look" to acknowledge my own admiration for the postwar French designer. The dramatic fuchsia coat, with its multicolored lining and matching dress, which she borrows for the occasion from Rose's closet, was Midge's very calculated idea of "dressing the part" for her role in court—as if for a scene in a movie rather than a serious but conventional situation. "I always dress nicely for important meetings," as she says with rather understated assurance to her lawyer.

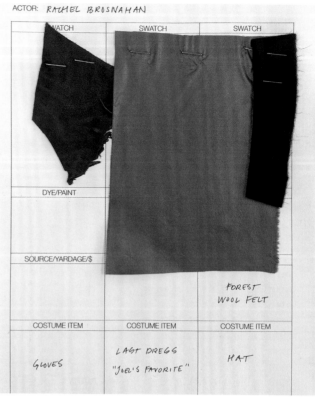

ACTOR: RACHEL BROSNAHAN

SWATCH	SWATCH	SWATCH
DYE/PAINT		
SOURCE/YARDAGE/$		
		FOREST WOOL FELT
COSTUME ITEM	COSTUME ITEM	COSTUME ITEM
GLOVES	LAST DREGS "JOEL'S FAVORITE"	HAT

104

"You got outfits picked?" —SUSIE

It is Susie who introduces Midge to her own downtown patch—Greenwich Village and the Gaslight—then, as Midge's newfound guide and manager, the backstage world of variety theater in general—the Copacabana, the comedy clubs, the strip club, and the theater world of comedienne Sophie Lennon. And while Midge already had a theatrical tendency in her wardrobe choices, her encounters with this brave new world of performance increasingly impact her sense of identity onstage and off. Just as Mrs. Maisel the "mad divorcée" becomes Mrs. Maisel the stand-up comic, the theatrical "Mrs. Maisel" is reshaping the real-life character and many new looks of Midge.

"I'll add some gloves to this. That should give it some 'zazz." —MIDGE

Costuming explicitly for the theater in these scenes presented a marvelous—*madly* marvelous—opportunity to design a wide variety of performers from the period, especially women— the Copacabana chorus line, the strippers, Sophie Lennon. And when Midge peers through the round service-door window at the stage of the Copacabana, she imagines *herself* performing there in a fleeting, aspirational vision for which I chose a white, opalescent beaded dress to create a ghostly, glowing, ethereal image that communicates both glamour and otherworldliness.

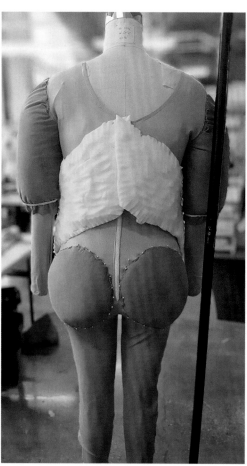

 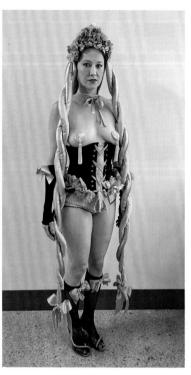  

The big Copa production number, one of the first major dance sequences in the series, featured showgirls in lavish, Latin-inspired costumes made with beaded metallics, lamés, and blush pink feathers. The dazzling Copacabana contrasts sharply with the strip club in episode 108, where the costumes were meant to look improvised, even homemade, with a somewhat vaudevillian edge. Midge's blue dress there, a mixture of reflective and matte blue silks and wools with blue-striped details, intended to be her performance look before her act was abruptly cancelled, is deliberately contrasting and demure, even schoolgirlish, vis-à-vis the revealing, outré costumes of the strippers.

"A fat suit is very warm, by the way." —SOPHIE

But the main attraction in this array of female performers is Sophie Lennon, played by Jane Lynch, whose extravagant, larger-than-life persona "Sophie from Queens" becomes the catalyst and then foil for Midge's own onstage persona "Mrs. Maisel." The real-life Sophie hides her sophistication beneath a multilayered foam fat suit and a simply patterned housedress, with the conviction that, for a female comic, the only viable route to success is parody, and so her stage persona is a homely, unattractive, vulgar clown. When Midge challenges and publicly rejects this premise onstage at the Gaslight—as well as what she considers Sophie's hypocrisy—it becomes one of the turning points of the series.

"Red works great with pink." —MIDGE

Midge decides to wear a red dress—*the* Red Dress—for Yom Kippur primarily as a provocative, rebellious challenge to Joel, but the scarlet vibrancy of the silk then also enables her to project and sustain an image of fearless audacity on her journey from the uptown family dinner to the Gaslight to, ultimately, jail. For me, the Red Dress scenes comprise one of the most decisive sequences in the unraveling of her previously one-sided, pseudo-perfect reality. And at the Gaslight, the Red Dress became one of Midge's most iconic impromptu performance looks, clinching her wholehearted embrace of comedy as a vehicle for blurring the lines between real life and performance.

110

SFA10 | 010
CHERRY

CHAPTER 07

The Garment District

"Love to hear the sound of the machines."
—MOISHE

In the 1950s, New York's Garment District was a very crowded world—in our case, Moishe and Shirley's crowded world. The shops were like layered beehives, with swarms of drapers, sewers, and tailors wedged into narrow spaces producing garments that would often become new fashions. And the search for an equivalent, contemporary setting led the production to one of the last, still functioning tailoring workrooms in Brooklyn, where many of the current staff were promptly enlisted as extras!

Costuming actual garment workers added a uniquely authentic look to our scenes and made for a great adventure, since I sent a contingent of my crew into the workroom with racks of period clothes to fit the working staff between breaks. I had done a great deal of research, of course, and was particularly inspired by the relatively obscure 1957 film *The Garment Jungle*, which suggested a number of interesting costume details—the handknit sweaters on the women, the inventively shaped headscarves fashioned from handkerchiefs on the men, and the dramatic look of clothing models wandering half-dressed among the sewing tables covered with paper patterns and bolts of cloth.

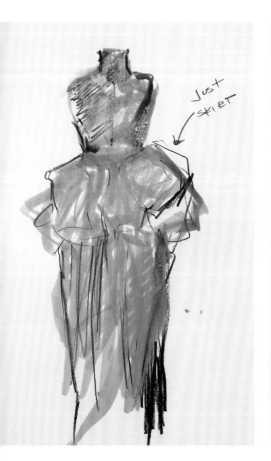

"I said halter. That's a sweetheart."
—MOISHE

Beneath the designs in progress, our models often wore a combination of period lingerie, billowing petticoats, and large, oversize bows that sometimes ended up on their heads as hair ornaments (!). Designing the models' deconstructed clothing from rolls of brightly colored silks was one of the most enjoyable aspects of costuming these extras for me—and actually an accurate portrayal of the practice of the period, when nameless designers often worked side by side in the shops with seamstresses and tailors. I produced sketches of the models as a starting point and then encouraged the drapers to loosely interpret the sketches themselves—which in fact turned out to be rather challenging, since they were being asked to drape dresses that would never be finished and had no final design!

"That roll of pink tulle you're dragging across the ground—it's French. Do you know what else is French? The guillotine!"
—MOISHE

The royal couple in this kingdom of machines and fabric were Joel's father Moishe and mother Shirley, played by Kevin Pollak and Caroline Aaron. I created a well-tailored but somewhat flashy image for Moishe. As "the boss," Moishe would dress as distinctly as possible from the workers, so I often built his suits from silk and wool blends in light creamy tones, which, when combined with his many gaudy tie clips, cufflinks, and ties, gave him a slightly ostentatious edge. And so I spent many mornings with Kevin, tête-à-tête, mulling over the choice of clip for Moishe's tie du jour.

But while Moishe was *somewhat* flamboyant, Shirley was a living, breathing hyperbole, and her boldly patterned wardrobe was deliberately excessive in its gaudiness. As Caroline and I repeated over and over during her fittings, Shirley's mantra was, "Never enough!" Her appetite for accessories was insatiable, and she always had to be armed—to the teeth!—with a necklace, a pin, a pair of big, crazy earrings, and a brightly colored handbag.

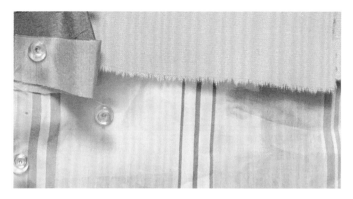

"You need a dress?" —MOISHE

"Always . . ." —MIDGE

The Garment District exteriors were among the biggest scenes we did in the show. And the sight of masses of workers steering racks of clothing through the streets to trucks that were receiving them by the dozens really epitomized this vibrant, colorful world that was such a significant part of New York City culture at the time. We first see this teeming street scene in the tracking shot in episode 102 that follows Joel's arrival in the Garment District to visit his father at Maisel & Roth, and then again in episode 308, when Midge essentially duplicates Joel's passage through the area for a meeting with Moishe herself.

We plotted Midge's path very carefully in season three by studying the footage from season one to try to echo every moment with our extras as the camera tracks Midge from the bustling street into and through the equally busy shop. In one of her most noted looks, Midge wears a light pink swing coat over a pale striped sundress with a multilayered hat of pastel chiffons that reminded me of puff pastry. I especially wanted this costume to exude a wildly optimistic energy as she dodges her way through the scores of colorful garment racks and the brisk but stolid workingmen that peopled the Garment District in the mid- to late 1950s. With, of course, the familiar romantic feeling of empowerment that only the inimitable Midge can bring to a scene.

CHAPTER 01

Clothes at Work: B. Altman

*"Going to bring the flats
tomorrow. That's the key. Flats."*
—MIDGE

B. Altman & Co., the legendary department store, was the arena in which Midge would strive in her own special way to embrace both the reality of the workaday world and the fantasy (!) of being a working woman as portrayed in 1950s films and advertising. I was personally inspired by Rosalind Russell's look for Mame's brief stint as a salesgirl at Macy's in *Auntie Mame* (1958), and was even explicitly thinking of her beautifully tailored blue dress when I designed Midge's purple, blue-trimmed Altman interview outfit. Both Mame and Midge are trying, in their elegant but somewhat comically overstated ways, to project the importance of being an earnest (!) professional—an idealized, glamorous image of a serious working woman.

"Mascara, blink, blot, spritz, done." —MIDGE

Up to this point, Midge's wardrobe was a kaleidoscope of colors, but I didn't feel that either her up- or downtown palettes from season one were adaptable to the context of B. Altman. For the Altman makeup floor, where Midge is first posted, I decided to use multiple shades of gray as the salesgirls' base color, mixed with some navy blues and patterns—particularly polka dots, since, in my design scheme for B. Altman overall, I associated polka dots with the makeup counters and stripes with the switchboard room, her two principal scenes of activity there.

In truth, I love working with grays, since all the colors of the spectrum seem to be hiding in their coolness or their warmth, and the preponderance of grays allowed the customers' clothing to stand out from the background wash of the salesgirls' basically blue and gray ensembles. The makeup girls were like a theatrical chorus, in outfits that

I conceived of as a cross between schoolgirl and circus, with small, handmade corsages worn on their dresses— little red and blue silk flowers for every day, and festive red velvet ones for Christmas. And we built a number of periwinkle uniform smocks embroidered with the old B. Altman logo for the window display and cloakroom girls, which Midge also wears when she's temporarily exiled to the coat check room herself.

Midge's palette, then, needed to be consistent with that of the other girls—uniform to a degree, but without quashing or stifling her individuality. So if her outfits were more self-consciously understated than was her wont, they were still replete with perky, extra-feminine details like fancy silk bows and decorative collars and cuffs and subtle pink trim. And as we transitioned from season one to two at B. Altman, though I was still primarily working with shades of gray, I introduced more color variation into Midge's clothes, dressing her in a gray*ish* green suit for Christmas at the end of season one.

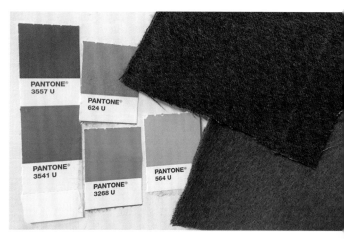

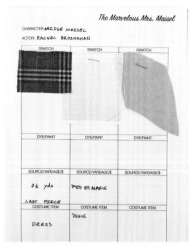

The Marvelous Mrs. Maisel

CHARACTER: MIDGE MAISEL
ACTOR: RACHEL BROSNAHAN

SWATCH	SWATCH	SWATCH
DYE/PAINT	DYE/PAINT	DYE/PAINT
SOURCE/YARDAGE/$	SOURCE/YARDAGE/$	SOURCE/YARDAGE/$
7½ yds	DYED BY MARIE	
LAST PIECE		
COSTUME ITEM	COSTUME ITEM	COSTUME ITEM
DRESS	DICKIE	

AS ABOVE, NOT SO BELOW

The makeup department and the switchboard room at B. Altman were essentially opposing worlds: the quietly sophisticated first-floor heaven of lipstick and blush, and the manic basement hell of the telephone switchboards. When I first looked at research photos of switchboard operators in the 1950s, my initial, strange impression was that many of them were wearing stripes—and because I was already thinking of the switchboard room as an underworld, this is what first prompted me to use stripes below as a counterpoint to the more celebratory, circus-like polka-dot theme on the floor above.

But despite her shuttling back and forth between polka dots and stripes, Midge never really relinquishes her predilection for grays at B. Altman, even during her penitential period at the switchboard—an expression, perhaps, of her dream of an eventual return to the makeup heaven above. In general, however, the switchboard girls wore somewhat earthier tones than the salesgirls—olives, rusts, golden browns, deep purples, and maroons—which provided more color and gave a somewhat warmer, cheerier feeling to their underground world. And when we first see Midge at the switchboard—at the beginning of season two—she appears to be making an effort to assimilate, in brick red and maroon, colors quite distinct from what we've seen her in previously.

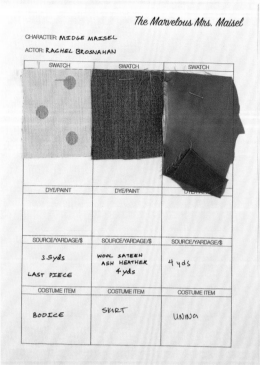

The Marvelous Mrs. Maisel

CHARACTER: MIDGE MAISEL

ACTOR: RACHEL BROSNAHAN

SWATCH	SWATCH	SWATCH
DYE/PAINT	DYE/PAINT	DYE/PAINT
SOURCE/YARDAGE/$	SOURCE/YARDAGE/$	SOURCE/YARDAGE/$
3.5 yds LAST PIECE	WOOL SATEEN ASH HEATHER 4 yds	4 yds
COSTUME ITEM	COSTUME ITEM	COSTUME ITEM
BODICE	SKIRT	LINING

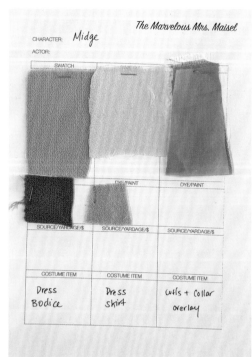

The Marvelous Mrs. Maisel

CHARACTER: Midge

ACTOR:

SWATCH		
	DYE/PAINT	DYE/PAINT
SOURCE/YARDAGE/$	SOURCE/YARDAGE/$	SOURCE/YARDAGE/$
COSTUME ITEM	COSTUME ITEM	COSTUME ITEM
Dress Bodice	Dress skirt	Cuffs + Collar overlay

NO WORK WITHOUT PLAY

Although her banishment from the makeup floor was clearly a demotion, the switchboard room became even more of a lovefest for Midge and her coworkers. Already in season one, they'd developed an after-hours social life that included several house parties, where, because the directors wanted a more conventional, fun, young '50s feeling, I used what I consider to be more classic '50s girly looks for Midge's off-duty peers—tight little colored sweaters, slim trousers, fuller skirts, and flats. And since Midge herself often went to extremes to make a splash with her outfits, I thought it would be amusing—and apt—to let her go a little over the top with her party looks here.

One idea came from an early Danskin ad for matching colored tights and shorts that was surprisingly advanced for 1959. I used it as the inspiration for Midge's *most* adventuresome party outfit, working with a variety of oranges and pinks—and for the first time, corduroy!

To a dressier party, Midge wore a Dior-inspired, pink silk and chiffon dress, once again borrowed from Rose's closet, that I called her "tutu look." Like the bottom of a bell-shaped romantic tutu, the skirt was constructed from many layers and shades of pink chiffon to achieve a fanciful contrast of color and texture, and it was worn with a richly beaded bolero top.

Midge's last off-hours social event with her Altman friends was her coworker Mary's Irish Catholic wedding, for which I designed a very pale pink silk dress and hat, deliberately echoing the flashback look in which she herself was a newlywed being carried over the threshold. In both costumes her "hat" is a fascinator, a kind of headpiece I've used frequently for Midge—like to accompany her yellow Catskills arrival dress—and here its playful shape is meant to add contrast to the bittersweet turn the scene will take at the end.

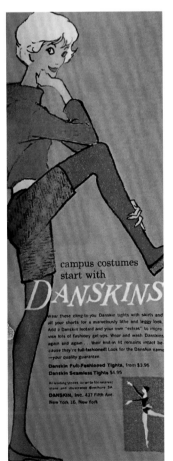

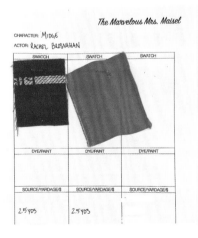

CHAPTER 02

La Vie en Rose

"One minute you're in New York,
and the next you're here in Gay Paree."
—ROSE

"Paris is always a good idea," Audrey Hepburn is supposed to have said in *Sabrina*, so for *Mrs. Maisel*—of course!—Paris was a *marvelous* idea.

Paris! What can I say . . . the most romantic city in the world! And in addition to being marvelous just to be there, a location that would have a massive impact on the characters and their costumes, in particular Rose and Abe.

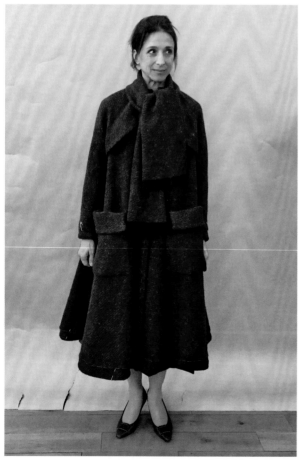

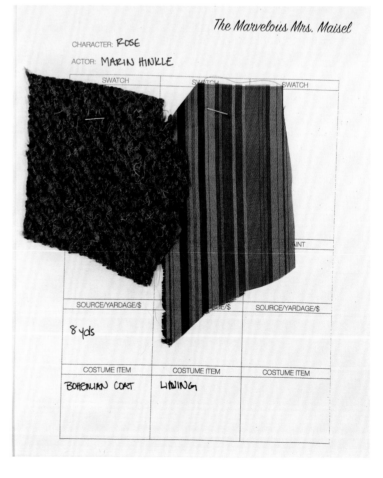

The Marvelous Mrs. Maisel

CHARACTER: ROSE

ACTOR: MARIN HINKLE

SWATCH	SWATCH	SWATCH
	PAINT	
SOURCE/YARDAGE/$	SOURCE/YARDAGE/$	SOURCE/YARDAGE/$
8 yds		
COSTUME ITEM	COSTUME ITEM	COSTUME ITEM
BOHEMIAN COAT	LINING	

RUNAWAY ROSE

In Paris, Rose discards her prim Chanel suits and pleasant, period pastels for an edgier, more daring look that I liked to call "schoolgirl bohemian." Having once studied in Paris myself at the École des Beaux-Arts, I had very vivid memories of deep-toned garments worn with purple flowing scarves, exotic turbans, and of course, berets—so many variations on a romantically shabby style that transcends decades.

And I remembered having seen a particular coat at a Dior exhibit that somehow captured the spirit of what I wanted to do for Rose—if I could just create a similar version in the beautiful shade of purple that haunted my memories. . . . I decided to build the coat—and then the rest of Rose's wardrobe—at a costume shop in Paris I'd discovered many years earlier while working there on an independent film. But finding a fabric of just the right texture with just the right color proved to be extraordinarily tricky. Only after creating a seemingly endless number of dye samples, when we succeeded in producing that elusive Paris purple hue, did I know we were on our way to creating a novel Paris look for "runaway" Rose.

With the coat as a point of departure, then, because of its unconventional shape and texture, I proceeded to create a series of jumpers that could be schoolgirlish and sexy at the same time—a nod to Audrey Hepburn at the beginning of *Funny Face*, a film I looked at often for Parisian inspiration. In addition to the jumpers, I used turtlenecks, sweaters, and jewelry that would be most at home in the more bohemian Latin Quarter of Paris. And at the flea market I found several strongly graphic pieces of jewelry, an original Jacques Fath scarf, and a traditional market basket that was identical to the one I'd carried every day to the Beaux-Arts filled with my art supplies.

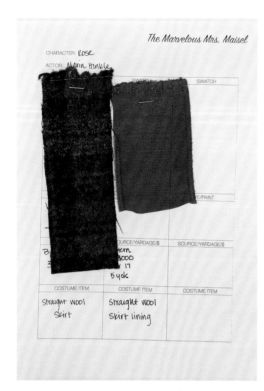

The Marvelous Mrs. Maisel

CHARACTER: Rose
ACTOR: Marin Hinkle

COSTUME ITEM: Straight wool skirt
COSTUME ITEM: Straight wool skirt lining

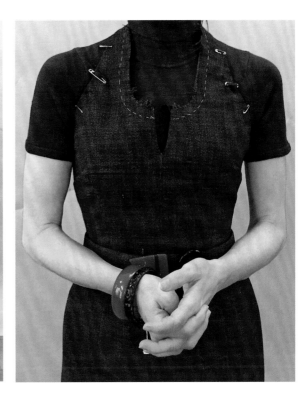

The Marvelous Mrs. Maisel

CHARACTER: Rose
FOR: Marin Hinkle

	DYE/PAINT	DYE/PAINT
SOURCE/YARDAGE/$	SOURCE/YARDAGE/$	SOURCE/YARDAGE/$
yds		PV-2000-159 3 yds
COSTUME ITEM	COSTUME ITEM	COSTUME ITEM
ight wool skirt		Straight wool skirt lining

I also hoped to make Rose's last, farewell-to-Paris costume, a hooded suit, one of her most dramatic looks. The colors—blood red, white, and powder blue, a playfully subtle allusion to the French flag—were meant to reinforce her emotional response to giving up Paris, liberty, and of course, her dog Simone. I wanted her to look like she was dressed for the finale of an old Hollywood melodrama, pulling up her hood as she leaves to give poignant punctuation to the scene.

But in spite of her departure, a new Rose was born in Paris. The dutiful New York wife had all but disappeared, and her clothing would continue to be freer, more adventurous, and even at times avant-garde.

"You don't recognize your own wife?" —MIDGE

The Rose effect, as I like to call it, also had a big impact on Abe, played by Tony Shalhoub. Up to this point, he always looked quite comfortably professorial—tweedily conservative, almost retro, and concerned with status quo in his own quirky way. But, like Rose, Abe had past ideals and aspirations, which are foreshadowed in his Paris looks though they only surface later in the season. After his initial display of reluctance, he progressively embraces the style of a Left Bank intellectual and café habitué—with a Basque beret, an indispensable scarf, a surplus leather jacket, and a corduroy vest I modeled on an old French workman's *gilet.* And while in season one his shirts are all a sober white or slightly off-white, I started to introduce textured shirting fabrics in cooler colors, mainly blues and grays.

Abe, like Rose, rediscovers himself in a world that is both different and strangely comfortable—especially, in his case, in the café scenes, where the most fun part was creating the other members of his coterie, their clothing spanning a range from French workers' blues to dark bohemian hues, inspired by the gatherings of Sartre.

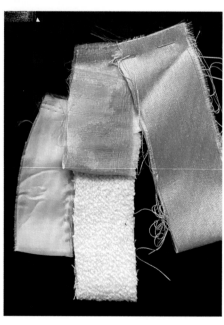

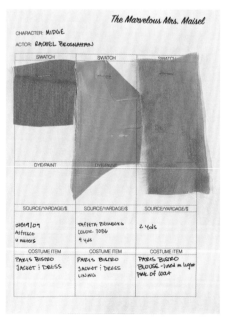

The Marvelous Mrs. Maisel

CHARACTER: MIDGE

ACTOR: RACHEL BROSNAHAN

SWATCH	SWATCH	SWATCH
DYE/PAINT	DYE/PAINT	DYE/PAINT
SOURCE/YARDAGE/$	SOURCE/YARDAGE/$	SOURCE/YARDAGE/$
31519/07 Alfresco 4 meters	TAFFETA BEMBERG COLOR 7056 4 yds	2 yds
COSTUME ITEM	COSTUME ITEM	COSTUME ITEM
PARIS BISTRO JACKET ¦ DRESS	PARIS BISTRO JACKET ¦ DRESS LINING	PARIS BISTRO BLOUSE - lined in light Pink of coat

WATER COLOR PATTER

"That other one in twelve shades of pink."
—MARIE

Midge, being forever Midge, had no choice but to find a pink plaid for what I called her "stewardess look." I extensively researched and eventually purchased a 1950s stewardess uniform, then juxtaposed the research on my design board with a photo from a vintage *Elle* of a model at an outdoor café with matching gloves and hat. Midge had never been on a plane, so I loved to imagine she'd seen a promotional picture of a stewardess, a particularly glamorous career in the 1950s, and thought, "Yes! *That's* how I should look!"

But finding a pink plaid fabric in the proper scale was a challenge. The one I thought could work had silver metallic threads running through it, so we had to remove them one by one, an extremely painstaking process, to create the perfect arrival look for the "one in twelve shades of pink," as Midge is referred to by the Paris concierge, Marie, played by Catherine Arditi.

Midge has two looks in Paris, and while the first is elegant but playful, I wanted Midge's second costume in Paris to be utterly, quintessentially romantic. I knew we would see the outfit in some of the most beautiful places in Paris by night, and so it was important to me that it literally seem to *glow* in the dark streets where we'd be shooting. I was thinking of Monet's *Water Lilies*, with splashes of soft pink over watery blues and greens, and so I designed a shimmery green satin suit over a sheer inner blouse (which we painted into—*à la Monet!*), worn under a silvery gray coat with rose-colored gloves and beret.

The overall feeling is meant to be melancholic and poetic, but the costume had to be seen in different contexts, as Midge wanders alone through the streets of Paris, then ends up appearing on stage with a trio of drag queens in dazzling beaded dresses. It needed to express all the exuberance yet poignancy of her brief Paris interlude, and I wanted it to be so *absolutely* Paris-appropriate that Midge not only seems at one with the beauty of Paris but could be the spirit of Paris itself.

"You can't run the world and have all the pretty underwear, too." —MIDGE

Capturing the spirit of Paris was equally important to me in costuming the day players and extras. Parisian culture and clothing were much more codified than in 1950s New York. So, for example, the prevalence of classic French workers' uniforms, from worn and faded to vibrant and new, made for an endless variety of indigoes and blues. For the other extras I mainly used deeper jewel tones, blacks, and dark browns, with color choices often inspired by ads in period magazines, where I often found myself just as enthused by the colors of cars and everyday household objects as of clothing.

Altogether, we costumed over a thousand extras in Paris, covering many locations. But perhaps the most challenging and fun extras to deal with were the performers at Madame Arthur's, reputedly the city's first drag cabaret, and therefore a great opportunity to present a lesser-known part of Parisian culture. But the men who were cast were unexpectedly muscular and tall, and I realized right away we would never find three beautiful dresses that would fit and convey the necessary allure. I'd imagined them beaded and sequined in deep red, pink, and silver tones, with beautiful wigs and fantastic high heels, emanating movie star—*French* movie star—mystique. So in the end, we had to build the dresses from scratch in the workshop with elaborate understructures to enhance hips, buttocks, and bust.

We also staged an ambitious dance on the quay below Notre-Dame, with more complex choreography than any in New York in season one. The dancers had to be dressed as evening strollers—realistically—but in costumes that could accommodate their dance moves and, in the women's case, skirts that would still look marvelous as the dancers were tossed in the air. Again, the palette echoed the jewel tones, reds, and purples that characterized my personal romantic vision of Paris.

CHAPTER 03

Borscht Belt Barbie: Clothes at Play

"It's the Catskills; you can't have too many clamdiggers."
—ROSE

For urban New Yorkers, summers in the Catskills were transparently escapist—a time outside of time, a time for play! And so, I thought, the costumes for the Catskills would have to be light, playful, and superlatively fun.

One of my first instincts was, "It's time to use yellow," thinking of Van Gogh's madly marvelous understatement, "How beautiful yellow is," regarding the sun! I'd pretty much resisted using vibrant, sunny colors in what had been, up to this point, the urban landscape of the series. But when Midge emerges from the room on Riverside Drive that's become her closet exclaiming, "We're going to the Catskills (!)," I wanted her to appear as a sunburst of yellow in the spirit of Van Gogh.

The dress in which she trumpeted their departure and later arrived at the Steiner Resort—wryly named for our Brooklyn studio—was a yellow-flowered extravaganza in layers of printed silk chiffon—and was, in fact, the first time I'd used a floral pattern for Midge. And to reinforce the celebratory impression that we were crossing a new threshold, I repeated the design of the crown-like fascinator she'd worn on her head as a newlywed with Joel—this one, though, made from lovingly pleated, yellow grosgrain ribbon.

PLAYTIME

The Catskills were like a magical playground where visitors could shed their urban personae for relaxed, often quite whimsical, sometimes fantastical looks and behavior. And a costume like the sundress with its hand-painted lampshade hat that Midge wears for her "boating date" with Benjamin, played by Zachary Levi, is a perfect example. The backless halter dress, which was built from multicolored vintage fabric, splits down the front to reveal a pair of moss green shorts, a take on a "playsuit" look that was popular in the late '50s. For the period, it was daring and was even meant, in this context, to be borderline provocative for her first, contrived date with Benjamin.

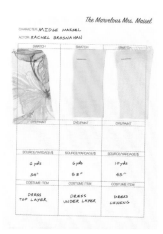

The Marvelous Mrs. Maisel

CHARACTER: MIDGE MAISEL
ACTOR: RACHEL BROSNAHAN

SWATCH	SWATCH	SWATCH
DYE/PAINT	DYE/PAINT	DYE/PAINT
SOURCE/YARDAGE/$	SOURCE/YARDAGE/$	SOURCE/YARDAGE/$
6 yds	6 yds	10 yds
54"	52"	45"
COSTUME ITEM	COSTUME ITEM	COSTUME ITEM
DRESS TOP LAYER	DRESS UNDER LAYER	DRESS LINING

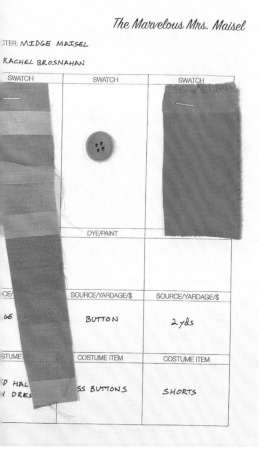

The Marvelous Mrs. Maisel

...CTER: MIDGE MAISEL

...RACHEL BROSNAHAN

SWATCH	SWATCH	SWATCH
		DYE/PAINT
...CE/	SOURCE/YARDAGE/$	SOURCE/YARDAGE/$
...GE	BUTTON	2 yds
...STUME	COSTUME ITEM	COSTUME ITEM
...D HAL... ...DRES...	...SS BUTTONS	SHORTS

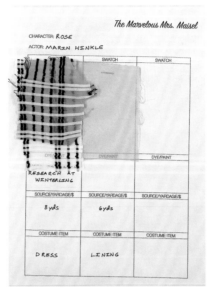

The Marvelous Mrs. Maisel

CHARACTER: ROSE
ACTOR: MARIN HINKLE

SWATCH	SWATCH	SWATCH
DYE/PAINT	DYE/PAINT	DYE/PAINT
RESEARCH AT WINTERLING		
SOURCE/YARDAGE/$	SOURCE/YARDAGE/$	SOURCE/YARDAGE/$
8 yds	6 yds	
COSTUME ITEM	COSTUME ITEM	COSTUME ITEM
DRESS	LINING	

The Marvelous Mrs. Maisel

CHARACTER: MIDGE MAISEL
ACTOR: RACHEL BROSNAHAN

SWATCH	SWATCH	SWATCH
DYE/PAINT	DYE/PAINT	DYE/PAINT
SOURCE/YARDAGE/$	SOURCE/YARDAGE/$	SOURCE/YARDAGE/$
2 yds 60"	2 yds 60"	
COSTUME ITEM	COSTUME ITEM	COSTUME ITEM
HALTER TOP	SHORTS	2" BELT + 1.5" BELT SHERRY

"My God, you look like sisters." —EDIE

The theme of self-conscious playfulness—the fun factor!—is a thread that runs through most of the costume choices in the Catskills, and translated, for Midge and Rose, into a pattern of "complementary pairing"—like in the ping pong scene, for which I designed a checked, scalloped halter top and green shorts with a bright yellow belt for Midge, and a coordinating lime-green chiffon wrap dress with a yellow underlayer for Rose.

But their impulse to coordinate reached its peak in the hair salon scenes, where they wear smocks of different colors but identical pattern and texture. Determined to find the *most* utterly fetching fabric that wouldn't stretch credibility as a salon smock, I located an unusual fabric from France that had a strange, wax-like surface and a seductive floral print in two different colors—extravagant, but too perfect to resist!

In the same spirit of casual fun, for their bicycle ride, Midge's blue headscarf and short blue capris—or literally, in this case, pedal pushers—are juxtaposed with a folk-inspired costume for Rose, who wears a *red* scarf and an inversely voluminous denim skirt. And for the birdwatching scene, I started with two dramatically funny straw hats and added colorful skirts, which, in Midge's case, resembled a romantic version of camouflage. Together they made me think of a madcap butterfly safari.

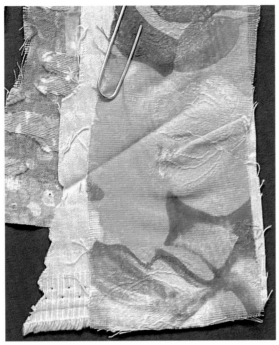

Rainbow strips of fabric and radical juxtapositions of color characterize a number of their costumes, like Rose's bright silk panel dress at the welcome dance and her more pastel-hued dock dress. Or Midge's boat-date sundress and the more graphically adventurous outfit she wears for "Simon Says," where I combined a purple plaid linen skirt with a bright floral cotton top for a deliberately atypical, less predictable mix of patterns.

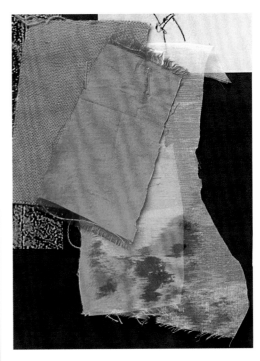

In general, this being the first time in the series that I designed for summer, I used a lot of linen and cotton and many more sheer fabrics in the costumes. One of my favorites, which combines both summer linens and floral sheers, was the persimmon ensemble Midge wears for the meteor shower. It resembles her yellow arrival dress in its commitment to multiple monochromatic, sheer, patterned layers, and I tried to achieve a similar painterly quality in the blend of various orange and apricot tones.

167

"So this year, should I go classy? Or risqué?" —MIDGE

This is also the first time we see Midge in a bathing suit. For the bathing beauty contest, the directors decided they wanted her in a bikini—her "Mamie Van Doren," or "risqué" versus "classy" swimsuit look—which I chose to build in polka dots to emphasize the edge of zaniness even in Midge's slightly sexier choices. It also allowed her bikini to stand out from the parade of primary-colored, one-piece swimsuits in the scene. My idea was to put all the other women on the dock in distinct, solid hues against the backdrop of the lake for a broad spectrum of color with Midge at the center.

Then, for the later dock scene, Midge "goes classy" in the white, Grecian-style bathing suit I modelled on the swimsuit worn by Grace Kelly in *High Society* (1956), a suit that Rachel and I both loved—although in the end, to our regret, the scene was abridged and it had very little screen time.

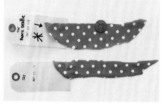

"You saw me in my romper, didn't you?" —ABE

Abe's appearance in his retro romper, or jumpsuit, was another one of the Catskills' memorable images. Looking for an example of a believable but comic exercise outfit for Abe, I was particularly drawn to the look of the popular television exercise guru Jack LaLanne, whose pioneering workout program began in the early '50s. In his stretch jumpsuit and ballet slippers, he looked like a cross between a gymnast and a French mime. For Abe, to give his romper a special character, I experimented with various graphic patterns from men's period sport shirts, then adapted the chosen design to the skintight line of the jumpsuit. Coupled with Tony's brilliant improvisations, the romper seemed to take on a droll identity of its own. As Shirley put it, "We've all seen Abe in his little romper; it's hysterical." "And so formfitting," added Moishe.

"She doesn't look professional. She was carrying a toilet plunger." —ABE

For the palette of the Steiner Resort's staff uniforms, I initially appropriated the trademark salmon and blue of a mid-century Howard Johnson's (!), and repeated that color combination in uniform skirts, blouses, trousers, shorts, and jackets according to each employee's function and status. But after creating numerous variations on this bicolor theme, the striped coverall—like the one accessorized by Susie with her indispensable plunger—was for me the supreme incarnation of the signature Steiner look.

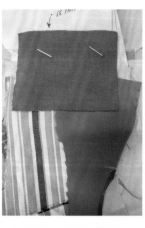

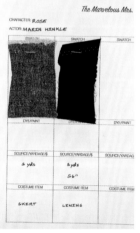

The Marvelous Mrs.

CHARACTER: ROSE
ACTOR: MARIN HINKLE

CORRECT
SIDE

WRONG
SIDE

"I think, next year, it's going to be time for a new grass skirt." —ROSE

But the greatest opportunities to create the kind of fanciful, theatrical clothes that flourished in the Catskills were the resort's annual luau, or "Polynesian Night," and the staff's farewell revue, "Around the World in 80 Minutes."

For Polynesian Night, I amassed an abundance of flowers and leis, straw skirts, and botanical fabrics, especially for Abe, Rose, and the Maisels. And I particularly loved working on this scene with Caroline Aaron, balancing her character Shirley's chronic overindulgence in accessories with the incongruous fur coat that was so essential to her image in the Catskills.

Then the Around the World pageant that concluded the Catskills sequences proved to be a marvelous opportunity to create an amusing assortment of looks inspired by

international folk costumes. For each number, I selected a few choice elements that were iconic to each location—at least from the often stereotypical viewpoint of the '50s—and processed them through a vaudevillian lens.

The costumes of the Scottish highland dancers, then, were collaged from at least six different plaids; the Dutch cloggers from layered aprons, wooden shoes, and an exaggeratedly wide-winged Volendam hat; the Peking Opera-inspired Chinese from a profusion of silk ribbons, streamers, and pompoms—and so on for the high-kicking Cossacks, Arabian snake-charmer, and Venetian gondolier.

And in designing the Brazilian number in which Susie appeared, I was thinking about the campy eccentricity of the sometimes generically "Latin" dance sequences of the '50s TV classic, *I Love Lucy*. So the costumes became more Cuban than Brazilian, and were all about striped trousers, bare midriffs, and ruffles galore.

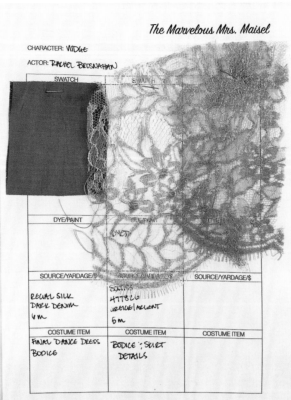

The Marvelous Mrs. Maisel

CHARACTER: MIDGE
ACTOR: RACHEL BROSNAHAN

SWATCH	SWATCH	
DYE/PAINT	DYE/PAINT	DYE/PAINT
	DYE?	
SOURCE/YARDAGE/$	SOURCE/YARDAGE/$	SOURCE/YARDAGE/$
REGAL SILK DARK DENIM 4 M	SULTISS 477826 GREIGE/ACCENT 6 M	
COSTUME ITEM	COSTUME ITEM	COSTUME ITEM
FINAL DANCE DRESS BODICE	BODICE + SKIRT DETAILS	

TRIPPING THE LIGHT

In addition to the many casual, playful daytime looks, there were more formal, elegant dresses for the opening and closing nights of the season. Midge's dress for the welcome dance was made in a pink vintage silk with an exuberant floral pattern to reflect the wide-eyed expectations of summer. Then, from an obverse perspective, her finale dress was made in muted shades of blue overlaid with silver appliqués. An ad for a popular perfume of the period, "Evening in Paris," had become my inspiration, so I wanted the dress to suggest a warm evening sky with glittering points of light. With the summer in the Catskills at an end, this dance, the farewell dance, was romantic but *very* melancholic, as it set the seal on Midge's definitive separation from Joel.

CHAPTER 04

It Came with a Hat: Witchcraft

"Your shoes match your purse. How did that happen?"
—BENJAMIN

"Witchcraft."
—MIDGE

Toil and trouble! Conjuring up the outfits for the romantic scenes with Benjamin did indeed require some very cunning, potent witchcraft!

I wanted each of the "date looks" to be striking and distinctly individual, while collectively presenting a newly adventurous side of Midge—charmingly seductive, with just the right, slightly fanciful edge of sexiness. And so, in keeping with her character, the black-and-white-checked short set she wears to travel into the city from the Catskills is meant to be enticing but not risqué, and is trimmed and accessorized with Midge's nostalgic, signature pink—cuffs, shirt, shoes, purse, and a headscarf that channels Grace Kelly. Midge in these scenes is, as ever, fully aware of her choices, but her intentions remain elusive, and there's a persistent undercurrent of innocence to her style.

For their theater excursion, Midge's first real date with Benjamin, I wanted to echo the red dress—*the* Red Dress—from season one, with its subliminal, strong sense of independence. But a cooler, *pinker* magenta gave the theater dress a softer feminine quality, and the matching shoes and purse that elicited Benjamin's comment above, already so familiar to us as typical of Midge, further enhanced her aura of alluring eccentricity for Benjamin. And so, when Midge brings this look—and Benjamin—to the Stage Deli, where for the first time she is incongruously overdressed, it highlights the significance of the moment as a romantic turning point.

"It came with a hat." —MIDGE

"All the great ones do." —BENJAMIN

Given my own painting background and having lived for many years in the East Village, I *loved* designing the downtown art world scenes—the gallery opening, the gathering at the Cedar Tavern (actually shot at McSorley's), and the ensuing visit to Declan Howell's studio. As a student, I'd even worked briefly in one of the last remaining galleries on East 10th Street, in the part of the East Village that, long before Soho or Chelsea, was the nexus of the artist and gallery scene in the 1950s.

For the gallery opening, then, I did even more extensive research on the downtown art world, where there was a boldness to people's clothing, often bordering on the avant-garde, that went beyond the basic beatnik styles of the Gaslight. For Midge, I anticipated the bubble shape I would use for her black silk performance dress at the telethon, since the bubble dress was unquestionably cutting-edge at the time. But here, for the gallery, I chose a bold black-and-white pattern with a floral motif of red poppies and, to make the poppies more abundant, appliquéd additional flowers, cut from excess yardage, onto the fabric. And then, to accentuate the interplay of color even further—it was, after all, the world of abstract expressionism!—I made her a vibrant, purplish indigo coat.

For the dress Midge wears the next day to Declan's studio, I had to cast another kind of charm. I'd worked with Rufus Sewell, who played Declan, before, and we'd looked at a lot of images of Francis Bacon and Lucian Freud in their studios for character inspiration. With Declan, then, in his torn, paint-spattered shirt, surrounded by brushes, rags, pots, easels, and half-finished paintings, I felt that Midge both needed to be conspicuous, yet harmonize with the creative background chaos. Ultimately one of my favorite costumes, the resulting matte, aqua-blue wool dress with a twisting, interwoven, shiny green silk sash, when completed with its bluish green coat and hat, made for a surprisingly magical moment for me. And it was, I think, effective in helping Midge to counterbalance Declan's formidable presence as a character.

The Marvelous Mrs. Maisel

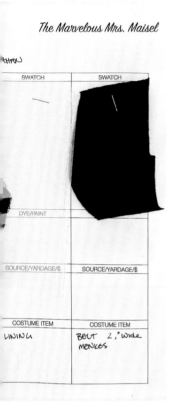

SWATCH	SWATCH
DYE/PAINT	
SOURCE/YARDAGE/$	SOURCE/YARDAGE/$
COSTUME ITEM	COSTUME ITEM
LINING	BELT 2" WIDE MENKES

The Marvelous Mrs. Maisel

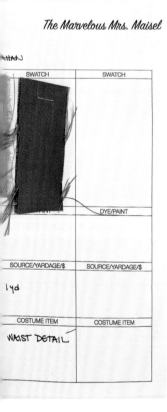

SWATCH	SWATCH
PAINT	DYE/PAINT
SOURCE/YARDAGE/$	SOURCE/YARDAGE/$
1 yd	
COSTUME ITEM	COSTUME ITEM
WAIST DETAIL	

CHAPTER 05

Deli Dressing: The Stage

"This place has the best pastrami, right?"

—*SUSIE*

The delis, or delicatessens, in the Manhattan theater district, like the rival Stage and Carnegie Delis, were inseparable from the culture of the New York entertainment world from the 1930s until they both closed in the early twenty-first century. And like its historic namesake, the Stage Deli in the show is a lively meeting place for denizens of the theater world, from stagehands to celebrities—not unlike a European café, but with a distinctive New York flavor perfectly represented by Verla the deli waitress, played by Peggy J. Scott, with her archetypically brash New York accent and manner.

The Marvelous

CHARACTER: MIDGE
ACTOR: Rachel Brosnahan

SWATCH	SWATCH	S
SOURCE/YARDAGE/$	SOURCE/YARDAGE/$	SOURC
8 YDS	Teal/7 YDS	
COSTUME ITEM	COSTUME ITEM	COS
#53-7 Garment #3 Blue/green plaid Topcoat	#53-7 Garment #3 Coat Lining	

"I thought there were going to be famous people here." —IMOGENE

Because virtually everyone in the entertainment business was eventually expected to turn up or pass through the Stage Deli, it came to serve as a perfect intermittent base for Susie and Midge in their efforts to connect with the showbiz community. The dress code was Midtown eclectic, and Susie customarily comes from the Village in her familiar Gaslight gear—cap, leather jacket, suspenders—her everyday working look until she starts to try, in her own quirky way, to look a little bit more like a "real" agent.

Midge's deli outfits, on the other hand, were conceived in one of two ways. Sometimes she dressed primarily for a rendezvous at the deli, as in the case of her meeting in season one with comedy writer Herb Smith—"writes jokes and eats pastrami"—played by Wallace Shawn, or the casual gathering in season three that is interrupted by Benjamin. But she more often appears at the deli en route to or from her other haunts—the Gaslight, B. Altman, the Upper West Side. And so, because these other costumes had to overlap at least one other principal scene, they were designed to be effective in more than one setting. Even the silk magenta dress Midge wore to the theater with Benjamin, her most "dressy" look at the deli, was conceived and designed for the theater date with the deli already in mind.

"Look at you; it's like a dollop of whipped cream grew a head." —SUSIE

Whenever Midge appears at the deli, either to meet Susie or other friends or agents or, in Herb's case, writers, I made a particular effort to heighten her color and give her a strong silhouette so that even when her costume would be straddling another scene, she still stood out distinctly from the deli's madding crowd.

And when she wears a hat, since she rarely removes it indoors, it is often the defining element of her look—like the plush, asymmetrical orange turban she wears to her meeting with Herb. I played with a variety of hat shapes at the deli, from a rust beanie to a green pillbox to a pink beret, making sure that, in each case, the hat would be a focal point of the outfit, since her image had to be powerful even when seated in a booth—which, in fact, was most of the time at the deli!

We first see Midge at the deli in an orange dress with a blue coat, and I returned to shades of orange for her last appearance there, when she's angrily, unexpectedly accosted by a jilted Benjamin. It's a potentially explosive, melodramatic situation, but she's wearing an outrageous kumquat flowered dress and a crazy, matching pillbox hat, an outfit sympathetic but amusing enough to accompany the acrobatics involved in clambering over a booth to confront him.

"Do not make me cry at the Stage Deli."
—*MIDGE*

Altogether, the principals and the extras at the Stage Deli represented a huge cross section of the New York types who populated Midtown, and they were among the most varied groups I costumed in the series. The front counter seats were typically filled with workers in coveralls, heavy boots, and twill jackets—essentially workmen on their breaks. And among the other regulars, I especially liked to focus on the off-duty comics and comedy writers, dressed in "normal" clothing with a subtly theatrical edge—like Wally Shawn in his windowpane checks and plaids—or the strictly business, showbiz types in their showy, slightly vulgar suits and ties.

The deli is an essential place to network. Agents meet clients and deals are made there, aspiring performers and writers plan future projects and scout opportunities there. It becomes *the* place where Susie and Midge often meet to dream and scheme about Midge's budding career, and where Susie starts to hone her skills as a manager. Situated in Midtown, more or less at a crossroads between their various other stomping grounds, the deli is a convenient and hospitable base—not only for a meeting, but a hot pastrami sandwich!

CHAPTER 06

How Many Drawers

"I even bought pink driving gloves.
I brought them with me."
—MIDGE

Right away, the idea of Midge and Susie on a road tour conjured up images of a wildly madcap buddy film and inspired me to want to develop a suitably witty road trip aesthetic in which, of course, Midge would consciously and adeptly dress the part.

In fact, Midge begins the trip in a pink-and-black windowpane suit and coat ensemble that had a somewhat casual, sporty feel, but was still urbane enough to be worn at the Stage Deli with Imogene, played by Bailey De Young. It's a costume that I thought of as transitional between Midge's more typical city looks and the kind of "rough and ready" styles she'd cultivate on the road. I wanted to make a bold choice, so I used a windowpane check that reminded me of classic British motoring clothes—but in pink! Two versions of the same pattern, in a light strawberry for the suit and a deep rose for the coat, worn over a hot pink blouse, created a study in pink that wound up becoming one of Midge's iconic looks, and was photographed for season three by the incomparable Annie Leibovitz.

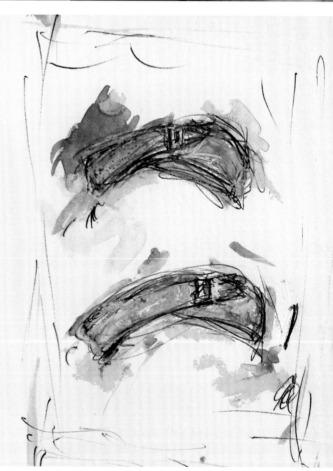

198

"How many drawers do you think you'll need?" —MIDGE

"Looks like one." —SUSIE

"Then I'll make do with the other five." —MIDGE

As might be expected, Midge does not travel light. Of course, she packs the requisite black performance dress for her bookings, though its relevance—and usefulness—diminish after she sleeps in it standing up. And though the remaining contents of her cases are never completely revealed, her subsequent outfits demonstrate her commitment to maintaining her self-image by looking fantastic—even in, by Upper West Side standards, rugged conditions. Tellingly, she even carries a hatbox with a selection of hats chosen carefully for each outfit. And a periwinkle negligee set, purposely more vibrant than her usual pastel nightwear, to enhance the comic impact of her motel bedtime scene in a facial mask.

"Who knows if they have irons where we're headed?" —MIDGE

At the gas station stop on the road from Washington, DC, where Midge's act was cut short by a backstage fire, we see her in the first of two examples of her idiosyncratic approach to fashion-conscious, rugged, on-the-road, outdoorsy attire. Since I felt that complementary colors would lend themselves well to the episode's spirit of new adventure, she wears a vivid outfit consisting of a pair of saffron orange shorts and top, under a cadet blue jacket and mustard yellow, buckled pillbox hat that suggest a peacoat and sailor cap.

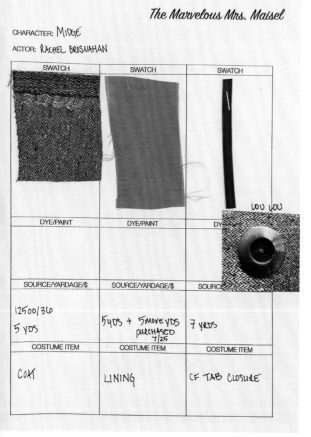

The Marvelous Mrs. Maisel

CHARACTER: MIDGE

ACTOR: RACHEL BROSNAHAN

SWATCH	SWATCH	SWATCH
DYE/PAINT	DYE/PAINT	DYE
		LOU LOU
SOURCE/YARDAGE/$	SOURCE/YARDAGE/$	SOURCE
12500/36 5 YDS	5 YDS + 5 MORE YDS PURCHASED 7/25	7 YRDS
COSTUME ITEM	COSTUME ITEM	COSTUME ITEM
COAT	LINING	CF TAB CLOSURE

"You're a comic, not Miss America. Just go on stage looking like shit."
—SUSIE

I continued the use of complementary colors for her other main road trip look— but more muted, with a chartreuse top over tapered, deep plum trousers. This second look spanned a few scenes, including one in which Midge got soaked in the rain—always a costume designer's nightmare!—and would ultimately become her impromptu performance look at the last stop on the tour. This progression was a major consideration when designing it, since I wanted to end up with a slender silhouette that echoed her early performance looks at the Gaslight. So, in fact, I worked backward from the Gaslight-inspired silhouette, heightening it with color and augmenting it with elements like an ochre loop-button jacket and Grace Kelly scarf. By the time that she returns completely bedraggled to New York, then, Midge—and her wardrobe!—have literally undergone trials by fire and by water, and she rushes on stage in a state of disarray only surpassed by her first appearance half-dressed at the Gaslight.

CHAPTER 07

Walking (& Talking) on Air

"I want a pink dressing room."
—MIDGE

Toward the end of season two, after a set of strategic—and hilarious—maneuvers in the Stage Deli, Susie secures a place for Midge on a telethon akin to the popular fund-raisers hosted by actor and comedian Jerry Lewis, whereupon Midge and Susie start to penetrate the brave new world of 1950s television. Television added a whole new medium to the previous panorama of performance possibilities for Midge, and for the first time in the series, I had to think like a 1950s designer myself about what her clothes would look like in both black-and-white and color.

Broadcast television was still young in the 1950s, and programs were created in an atmosphere of formality that has long since disappeared. In my research, I sometimes saw cameramen and studio crew in their shirtsleeves, but almost never without a tie. Even behind the camera, the overwhelmingly male majority of the crew wore suits. And as in many game shows of the period, the proceedings were conducted by a natty host flanked by a pair of comely—but mute!—assistants dressed in black-and-white beaded dresses.

Meanwhile, the on-camera entertainers were still primarily drawn from the world of theater, with a lineup like the roster of a variety show. I costumed clowns, cowboys and cowgirls, Shakespearean players, harlequin dancers, a French mime, glamorous starlets, a ventriloquist, baton twirlers, *two* Shirley Temple look-alikes—and, one of my favorites, a lion in a full fur suit. And though many of them looked like fish out of water in the studio, I assembled a choice cross section that I felt would be particularly amusing to see on the phone bank.

DOUBLE BUBBLE

Among the telethon's head-liners, Midge's nemesis Sophie Lennon performed another broad comedy skit as "Sophie from Queens," reprising her character's previous image, but going even farther here with the mocking insincerity of her routine.

By contrast, Midge appears as her consistently ebullient, stylish self. Having already costumed her for the gallery scene with Benjamin in a bubble dress, a popular, cutting-edge style in 1959, I now designed an even more full-blown version, this time in black, for her telethon performance. It was made from an especially lustrous black Italian silk, but apart from the shape I opted to keep it free of decorative details. This was the dress in which Midge would try to reach her broadest audience to date, and in which she would meet Shy Baldwin, who was going to change her life, so I wanted it to be fashionable and fun, yet understated and seductive.

SHY AWAY

We first see Shy Baldwin, played by Leroy McClain, the preceding day at the soundcheck in a casual look inspired by early images of Johnny Mathis, on whom the character was in fact partially based. His costumes would have a relaxed, straightforward elegance, and like the young Johnny Mathis, Shy displays a tendency to match his shirts with ties in pale, creamy colors for a monochromatic effect. In general, his palette was warm, particularly for his sweaters and casual trousers—and golden, as I pushed his performance look into subtly iridescent fabrics, an approach that would evolve in future episodes.

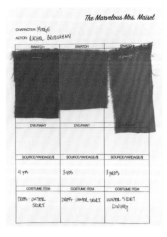

ALL ALONE

For me, the telethon sequence is easily one of the most affecting in the series. Then, in the following episode, which concludes the second season, we revisit the world of television with another unabashedly moving segment that peaks with the haunting appearance of actor Luke Kirby as Lenny Bruce on *The Steve Allen Show* performing "All Alone."

In terms of emotional impact, I feel there are times when a costume can play an operatic role—and for me, the finale of season two was precisely one of those moments.

For Midge's outfit in this sequence, I had a very strong feeling about combining three colors that had some

special resonance with her past. Midge's white coat is meant to evoke a cathartic feeling of transition here, and it's worn over a matching ivory blouse, a boldly passionate blood red skirt reminiscent of *the* Red Dress she wears in season one to the Gaslight, and a sash of the heroic green we first see when she bails Lenny out of jail.

We see her in this evocative outfit during a long sequence that encompasses her decision not to marry Benjamin, the sea change in Abe's career, her backstage visit to Lenny on air, Susie's reevaluation of her identity, and a last romantic interlude with Joel before she embarks on her own new, independent life on tour as an opening act for Shy. It was meant to convey a sense of life—*her* life—moving on, with the poignancy of farewell and great expectations for the future.

Red, White, Pink & Blue

CHAPTER 01

A Lot of Khaki: The USO Show

*"I could never be brave enough
to wear the same outfit every day."*
—MIDGE

From the early 1940s, and especially after World War II, USO shows—entertaining the troops—became a high-profile pursuit for entertainers of all stripes, including many comedians, not least because the pied piper of the USO was comedian Bob Hope.

And in order to fill a very large airplane hangar in New Jersey for our USO reenactment without resorting to CGI, we costumed over a thousand extras in period uniforms, which, I was told, broke—or at least rivalled—a New York record for the largest number of extras on set for a single day of shooting. "A lot of khaki," as Midge so aptly put it, and a daunting challenge for wardrobe. So, unable to build or find enough complete uniforms in the necessary time frame, we developed a system I liked to describe as resembling a Napoleonic battle formation, with the front lines perfectly costumed, successive lines less so—starting, of course, with shoes—until we reached the extras I called "shadow warriors," the farthest from the camera, who were dressed in just essential pieces, sometimes only shirts or T-shirts—but always dyed to the perfect shade of khaki!

Meanwhile, I thought of the tap dancers thronging the stage at the top of the scene as "Moulin Rouge Americana," with large, pink bow bustles that anticipate the red bow swag on Midge's own performance dress. I was playing with the idea of a red, white, and blue palette slyly filtered through a Parisian sensibility to color, in which salmon subs for red, periwinkle for blue, and black competes with white to ground the palette in a more 1950s burlesque, showgirl aesthetic. And fortuitously, since I didn't actually know that the camera would start the scene by focusing on the dancers' feet, I'd decided to daub a layer of showgirl glitter on each and every pair of shoes!

"This is the big leagues, kid. Got to start acting like professionals."
—SUSIE

This is the kickoff scene of season two, and it heralds Midge's emergence from the more parochial world of New York clubs into the "big wide world" of professional entertainment, opening for Shy Baldwin, a successful star who tours with an entourage that includes his own backup band, dancers, and handlers.

Her arrival costume, as if conceived by Midge herself, is, like her traveling "stewardess look," an example of her chameleon-like propensity to assimilate via her clothing, this time with a "military" look inspired by photos of Marilyn Monroe during a USO postwar tour of Korea in 1954. But instead of Marilyn's standard-issue olive green, I built a flyer's jacket for Midge in deep maroon, topped by a beanie with streamers of red, white, and blue—meant to show off the knack with which Midge can transform even army fatigues into fashion.

I also loved the feeling of Marilyn's period combat boots, and I simulated the look with a pair of contemporary French paratrooper boots, which are still close in form to midcentury US Army issue, but comparatively delicate. With a few buckle alterations, they complemented Midge's overall look, while adding a lighter, more feminine touch to a fairly tough ensemble.

"My goodness, that is a lot of khaki."
—MIDGE

For her performance dress, meant to be theatrically patriotic, I went for a truer palette of red, white, and blue than that of the dancers. I thought of Midge in her costume as a restless human flag of sorts with her big red bow trailing behind, long white evening gloves, and a pleated blue silk dress with multiple shades of blue underneath.

"Government cheese!"
—MIDGE

The blue underlayers themselves were very important, since they would be clearly seen when the dress billows up around her waist— yet another nod to Marilyn. My own department's prep for this shot that Reggie, played by Sterling K. Brown, would later dub the "panty pose," led to many amusing moments behind the scenes as we deployed a fan in the fitting room, testing different fabrics to find the one with the most effective lift and flutter.

SHY BLUES

I also kept to variations of blue in the costumes I designed for Shy and his backup singers. As with all of Shy's performance suits, I used wools that were interwoven with subtle iridescent threads. And to complement his look, I used metallic underlayers to add a shimmery glow to the backup singers' dresses in a lighter, airier blue.

In addition to the headliners like Shy—or, historically, Bob Hope or Marilyn—one of the more fascinating aspects of USO shows from the 1940s to the '60s was the eclectic array of other acts on the program. My own list included singing cowboys, jugglers, a country-clad hula-hooper, vaudevillian clowns, a sequined accordionist, and—of course!—Miss America. Extremely popular and often televised from the mid-1950s onward, these shows presented a wide-ranging cross-section of American entertainment, more often than not awash with effusive patriotism.

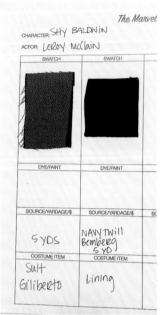

*"Blue dress,
blue dress."* —MIDGE

Though far more electric in tone, Midge's final USO look—for the canteen dance—conforms to the general palette of the episode with a vibrant blue dress that was partially inspired by a period Dior. But in keeping with the "wholesome" theme of the evening, it was also close in spirit to a fashionable prom dress. And I costumed all of the other girls in the scene in very voluminous, fluffy chiffon dresses meant to bounce and swing in time to their rapid, rambunctious dance moves.

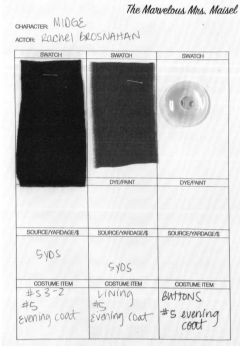

The Marvelous Mrs. Maisel

CHARACTER: MIDGE
ACTOR: RACHEL BROSNAHAN

SWATCH	SWATCH	SWATCH
	DYE/PAINT	DYE/PAINT
SOURCE/YARDAGE/$	SOURCE/YARDAGE/$	SOURCE/YARDAGE/$
SYOS	SYOS	
COSTUME ITEM	COSTUME ITEM	COSTUME ITEM
#S3-2 #5 evening coat	LINING #5 evening coat	BUTTONS #5 evening coat

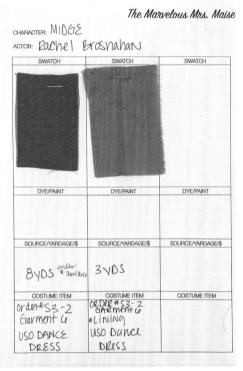

The Marvelous Mrs. Maise

CHARACTER: MIDGE
ACTOR: Rachel Brosnahan

SWATCH	SWATCH	SWATCH
DYE/PAINT	DYE/PAINT	DYE/PAINT
SOURCE/YARDAGE/$	SOURCE/YARDAGE/$	SOURCE/YARDAGE/$
8YDS order #764306	3YDS	
COSTUME ITEM	COSTUME ITEM	COSTUME ITEM
Order#S3-2 Garment Co USO DANCE DRESS	ORDER #S3-2 GARMENT Co *LINING USO DANCE DRESS	

"You sure you don't want to go home and grab your fancy blazer?" —MIDGE

Susie only seriously dresses *up* for the first time in the series to go to the party at Shy's house in Harlem, wearing one of the blazers that define her new identity as a now "professional" agent. So, to marshal Susie into the military theme of the canteen dance, I imagined that she'd won an oversize, double-breasted, olive-drab army trench coat during her gambling bout in the barracks. I always take great satisfaction in finding a simple garment that can amplify a character's physicality and expand a scene's intention, and this coat was exactly that type of garment for me. Also, in the back of my mind, I was thinking of the comic genius Harpo Marx in one of *his* many oversize coats, and that it would provide an amusing way for Susie to look both in and out of place at the dance.

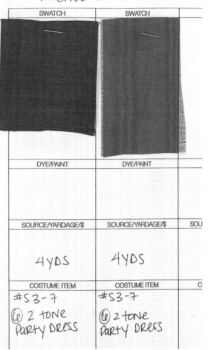

CHARACTER: MIDGE
ACTOR: Rachel Brosnahan

The Marvelo

SWATCH	SWATCH	
DYE/PAINT	DYE/PAINT	
SOURCE/YARDAGE/$	SOURCE/YARDAGE/$	SOU
4YDS	4YDS	
COSTUME ITEM	COSTUME ITEM	C
#S3-7	#S3-7	
© 2 tone Party Dress	© 2 tone Party Dress	

CHAPTER 02

Rose by Another Name

"And I don't want you without your clothes."
—ABE

Rose's looks in *The Marvelous Mrs. Maisel* basically straddle a tidy divide: Rose before
Paris and Rose after Paris; the Rose we think we know before and the Rose we *thought*
we knew after. Although there are some hints in season one as to where her journey
might be leading, it is only in the wake of the Paris escapade in season two that we really
feel we've embarked on a new direction with her costumes.

When I started to costume Rose after Paris, I often thought about how, without compromising her representation in season one, I could most effectively show the lasting
impact the Paris interlude had on her wardrobe. I wanted to develop a more *casually*
sophisticated way of approaching her character, and for inspiration, I started looking at
period clothes by designers like the American Claire McCardell in addition to the established couture names that sometimes influenced her earlier looks like Chanel.

The essence of the new, post-Paris Rose is first fully on display in her art class scenes
at Columbia University, where my goal was to let her Paris art student look morph into
a style that, while still moderately adventurous, could also pass for acceptable in the
Upper West Side world to which she'd returned.

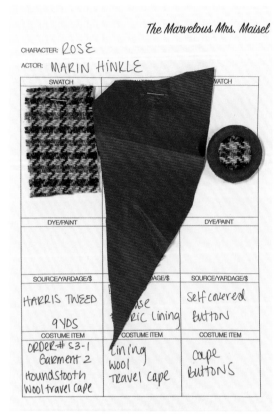

The Marvelous Mrs. Maisel

CHARACTER: ROSE
ACTOR: MARIN HINKLE

SWATCH		SWATCH
DYE/PAINT		DYE/PAINT
SOURCE/YARDAGE/$	AGE/$	SOURCE/YARDAGE/$
HARRIS TWEED 9 YDS	...se ...ic Lining	Self covered button
COSTUME ITEM	COSTUME ITEM	COSTUME ITEM
ORDER # S3-1 Garment 2 Houndstooth Wool travel cape	Lining Wool Travel Cape	cape buttons

RAMBLING ROSE

Beyond Columbia, the telltale signs of her new self-image were often subtle and focused on details or accessories like the avant-garde pieces of jewelry I now regularly paired with her ensembles. But sometimes she was more overtly flamboyant, particularly in her choice of outer garments like the extreme wrap coat she wore to Oklahoma, which would have been too outlandish for the more conventional Rose of yesteryear.

In Oklahoma as well, with two successive takes on a single outfit—a speckled blue tweed suit—we see a kind of summary illustration of Rose's evolution, from the old*est* to the new*est* Rose—the once and future Rose!—as she first evokes the image of her early life in cowboy hat and boots, then strides defiantly forward into the future in a spiraling, yellow ochre turban hat.

The Marvelous Mrs. Maisel

CHARACTER: ROSE
ACTOR: MARIN HINKLE

SWATCH	SWATCH	SWATCH
DYE/PAINT	DYE/PAINT	DYE/PAINT
SOURCE/YARDAGE/$	SOURCE/YARDAGE/$	SOURCE/YARDAGE/$
9 YDS	6 YDS	Vintage
COSTUME ITEM	COSTUME ITEM	COSTUME ITEM
ORDER # 53-1 Garment 3 DIOR Boucle Wool Suit	Lining	Buttons

227

EXOTIC ROSE

In the first season, I had already started making exotic headwear, especially structured turbans, a signature part of her wardrobe. Her predilection for turbans coincided with her practice of consulting urban fortunetellers who were arrayed in antique silk and velvet scarves and shawls, and even a crazy, pink-net, bird's nest hat from the 1960s that I'd found in my mother's collection. Rose embraced and thrived on these intimate storefront psychic encounters, and her turbans proclaimed her eagerness to engage in their immersive theatricality.

Then, in season three, as she begins to frequent the tearoom, where her matchmaking skills soon set her apart as a kind of seer herself, the tearoom sessions took the place of the visits to her dubious clairvoyants, and her range of headgear blossomed with luxuriant creations like the dramatic mint-green hat—of huge proportions!—that was worthy of a mad hatter.

CHARACTER: ROSE
ACTOR: MARIN HINKLE

	SWATCH	SWATCH
	DYE/PAINT	DYE/PAINT
SOURCE/YARDAGE/$	SOURCE/YARDAGE/$	SOURCE/YARDAG
#068 4YRDS	ES9100 col. 096 3YRDS	
COSTUME ITEM	COSTUME ITEM	COSTUME ITEM
S3-9 #3 DAY DRESS 308	S3-9 #3 INNER BIB (DBL LAYER) CUFFS (w/ WHITE BATISTE IN BTWN)	

CHARACTER: ROSE
ACTOR: MARIN HINKLE

		SOURCE/YARDAGE/$	SOURCE/YARDAGE/$
4 YRDS 40-			
COSTUME ITEM	COSTUME ITEM	COSTUME ITEM	
S3-8 #2 DRESS 308	S3-8 #2 BELT · 1ST CHOICE	S3-8 #2 BELT · BACK UP	

CHARACTER: ROSE
ACTOR: MARIN HINKLE

		D
SOURCE/YARDAGE/$	SOURCE/YARDAGE/$	SOUR
4 YRDS	2 YRDS	
COSTUME ITEM	COSTUME ITEM	CO
S3-9 #2 2 TONE DAY DRESS 308	S3-9 #2 CONTRAST WAIST BAND	

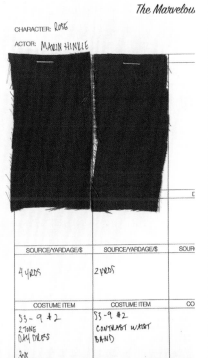

CHARACTER: ROSE

ACTOR: MARIN HINKLE

The Marvelou

SOURCE/YARDAGE/$	SOURCE/YARDAGE/$	SOUR
5 YRDS LAST!	2 YRDS + 1 YRD 1955	

COSTUME ITEM	COSTUME ITEM	CO
S3-7 #1 WOOL CREPE DRESS 307 S3-7 #2 JCKT	CONTRAST BOW & JACKET LINING	COVER OPTION CRE

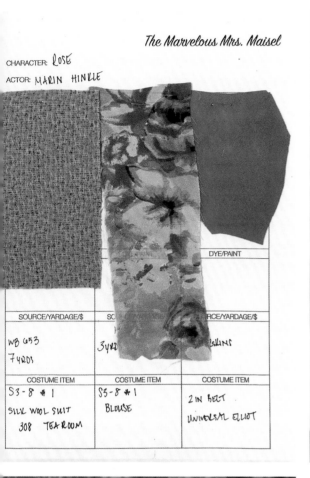

The Marvelous Mrs. Maisel

CHARACTER: ROSE
ACTOR: MARIN HINKLE

		DYE/PAINT
SOURCE/YARDAGE/$	SOURCE/YARDAGE/$	SOURCE/YARDAGE/$
WB 653 7 YRDS	3 YRD	ISKINS
COSTUME ITEM	COSTUME ITEM	COSTUME ITEM
S3-8 #1 SILK WOOL SUIT 308 TEA ROOM	S3-8 #1 BLOUSE	2 IN BELT UNIVERSAL ELLIOT

TEA ROSE

The tearoom excursions opened up a very magical world for me, and for Rose—a wizard of change!—as she became more comfortable in her new role as a match-maker psychic. I liked to think of the tearoom as a special place where women could bond, and historically, in fact, from the late nineteenth to mid-twentieth centuries, tea-rooms in the English-speaking world were often hotbeds of feminism.

Like the world of the fortunetellers but grander, the tearoom exuded its own kind of exoticism—like a lush conservatory garden, where I liked to think of the women themselves as hothouse flowers, botanical follies in headwear covered with blooms of all varieties. I used as many floral hats as possible to create an impression of endless arrays of brightly colored flower bouquets piled high on the heads of the tea-tasting ladies, resulting in a richly romantic atmosphere.

233

CHAPTER 03

From Gaslight to Limelight: Limelight Looks

"Wow." —SUSIE

"Good look?" —MIDGE

"The look." —SUSIE

In my earliest discussions with Amy and Dan about season one, the decision was made to complete Midge's costume arc at the Gaslight with an elegant black dress—and pearls—that became the first iteration of a kind of performance uniform. Then, over the course of the next two seasons, ruffles, swags, pleats, overlays, flares, lace, no lace, high waists, drop waists, bubbles, rhinestone buckles, and jeweled buttons all contributed to the growth of that first black Gaslight performance dress into a panoply of variations.

Designing those successive variations on a theme with ever new shapes and details was the tricky part. I did a seemingly endless number of sketches—sometimes building on previous looks with minor adaptations, sometimes treading more adventuresome paths. The key throughout was to maintain the basic concept of a credibly, potentially "normal" housewife in evening attire. The marvelous *Mrs.* Maisel wouldn't wear a gown as such, or anything *too* fancy or overloaded with decorative details, so I focused special attention on the qualities of the fabrics themselves, selecting them on the basis of their relative shine, transparency, opacity, or texture rather than color. Ultimately, I reasoned, this would allow each dress to have an identity of its own while still being part of a uni-*fied*, if not literally uni*form*, series.

BLACK TO THE DRAWING BOARD

In season three, I started to introduce some color accents into the sequence of "limelight looks," and though still restrained, it felt like a wildly radical departure. Tropical, vibrant Miami seemed a sufficiently uninhibited setting in which to let loose; so there, but not without trepidation (!), I added a first splash of color by trimming Midge's second Fontainebleau performance dress with boas—feathered and pink!—for a more fanciful, even whimsical impression.

Then, still in Miami, and in keeping with my predilection for green as Midge's heroic, "fearless" color, I twisted a green swag of silk into the black performance dress she wears to find a bruised and traumatized Shy hiding out on his boat—where, I felt, the puddling of the fabric, with its streams of green on the floor as she crouches to comfort him, reinforced the poetry of the scene.

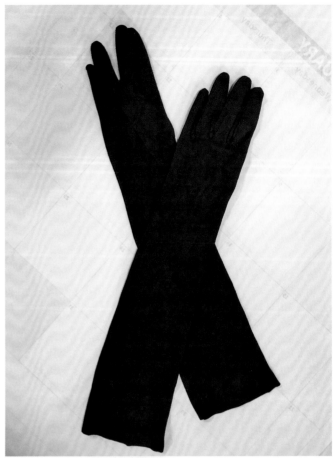

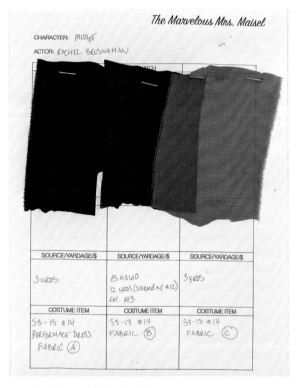

The Marvelous Mrs. Maisel

CHARACTER: MIDGE

ACTOR: RACHEL BROSNAHAN

SOURCE/YARDAGE/$	SOURCE/YARDAGE/$	SOURCE/YARDAGE/$
3 YRDS	854360 12 YRDS (Shared W/ #12) col. 143	3 YRDS
COSTUME ITEM	COSTUME ITEM	COSTUME ITEM
S3-13 #14 PERFORMANCE DRESS FABRIC Ⓐ	S3-13 #14 FABRIC Ⓑ	S3-13 #14 FABRIC Ⓒ

BLACK IN TIME

The shift into color reached its height at the end of season three with the pink sequined dress Midge wears for her appearance at the Apollo, her boldest color choice to date. Meanwhile, the procession of black dresses was meant to create continuity—with variety—for Midge's onstage persona. All of her limelight looks were quintessentially theatrical—and to me, they were the outward manifestations both of her dialogue with the world and the ongoing dialogue with herself about her identity as a performer.

CHAPTER 04

Road Mode: Las Vegas Glitz

"I've packed, unpacked, and repacked..."
—MIDGE

We accompany Midge on her dream tour with Shy Baldwin to its hottest spots—Las Vegas and Miami, two very distinct locations with two very different styles. So, although they were part of the same grand tour, I wanted to show that Midge, on stage and off, adapted her clothing to each locale.

Las Vegas was their first destination, and the flight to Las Vegas is actually the first time Midge boards a plane for "professional" purposes, so I designed her travel outfit to reflect a still somewhat ingenuous sense of excitement and enthusiasm. Her outfit, a baby blue coat lined with a delicate floral print over a cream skirt and blouse with a belt to match the coat's lining, was meant to convey a jubilant, celebratory feeling—as if to say, even if not the bride, she was part of the wedding party!

Similarly, the pale green and plum suit she wears to the press conference on arrival exudes a coquettish note of naïveté, with its guardedly conspicuous colors paired with what is basically a demure, but full-skirted silhouette for a buoyant, slightly girlish effect. And at other moments, like the scenes in which Midge and Susie run through the lobby to the marquee in their pajamas to see "their" name in lights, or later, again in pajamas, put on beauty masks in their room—an allusion to Midge's schooldays at Bryn Mawr—I wanted to reinforce the impression of girls at play, and the contrast between Midge's initially tentative poise on arrival and the gaudy, brash world of "big-time" Las Vegas.

COAT OO
PLANE

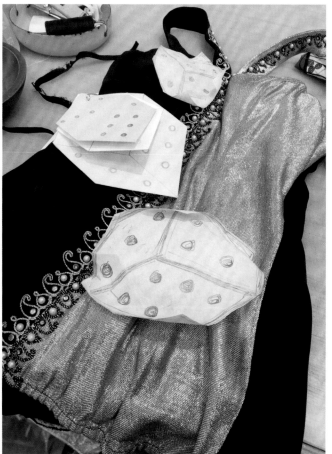

"It's the big time, baby."
—SUSIE

By the late 1950s, Las Vegas wasn't just another gambling resort, it was already unique in the world—and uniquely American. The more deeply I researched it, the more I realized the extent to which the imagery of Wild West Americana was inseparable from its identity. Except that in wild—but never woolly!—Las Vegas, the cowboys could as easily be mobsters.

And while gambling was its principal raison d'être, it was also a showcase for all sorts of glitzy, extravagant entertainment. And glitzy, extravagant people! I imagined the casinos of the 1950s thronged with golden showgirls, greeters dressed as human dice, and flashy patrons clad in as many glittery, bead-encrusted, and metallic fabrics as possible. Ultimately, then, my designs were as much concerned with the play of light on the clothes as with color, and I wanted the vast rooms of extras to shimmer with a luminescent glow—which, combined with elements of Western wear, became my secret recipe for concocting a distinctive Las Vegas atmosphere.

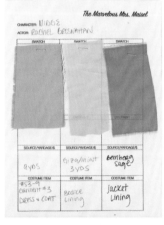

> ## *"Takes a while to get back into road mode."*
> —*SHY*

Shy and his band—established, experienced entertainers—reprised the previous elegance of their costumes, but with somewhat heightened formality, and they dressed in tuxedos on stage to acknowledge their sense of the venue's importance. But with Midge, I chose to introduce the features of her Vegas style more subtly and progressively.

Left: A black chiffon dress tying on one shoulder—asymmetrical—was a Givenchy collection kit—here, with a sliver of décolletage to the waist. $125. American copy: Lord & Taylor. *Above:* Another off-shoulder Givenchy dress has two bows—one at the shoulder, one

"This is not my normal 'do."
—*MIDGE*

The transition spans the sequence that transports her from insecurity to confidence onstage in the performance dress and out-of-character updo that distinguished her first appearance there. For this look, I always planned to attach an extremely large bow to the single shoulder of a black asymmetrical dress. Then, when the costume was made and the bow turned out to be larger—*much* larger—than expected, I realized it would be even better able to balance her outrageous, cone-like, beehive hairdo. So, by chance—Las Vegas luck?—there was a comic side to this dress that was much more pronounced than in any other of her performance looks, a gentle touch of humor that helped lighten the impact of Midge's bombed performance.

And then, as she rallies, Midge, in her endlessly adaptable way, displays more traces of sparkle in her wardrobe, with each of her subsequent limelight looks deferring to Las Vegas style with the presence of glittering rhinestones. And to celebrate the success of her connection with the Vegas vibe, I designed a special outfit for the phone scene in her hotel room filled with countless yellow teddy bears—the resplendent persimmon swing dress with its wide, gold metallic belt—her ultimate homage to the sway of casino culture.

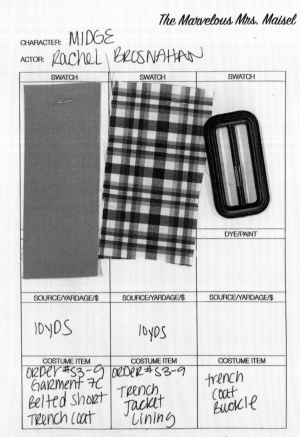

The Marvelous Mrs. Maisel

CHARACTER: MIDGE
ACTOR: Rachel BROSNAHAN

SWATCH	SWATCH	SWATCH
		DYE/PAINT
SOURCE/YARDAGE/$	SOURCE/YARDAGE/$	SOURCE/YARDAGE/$
10 YDS	10 YDS	
COSTUME ITEM	COSTUME ITEM	COSTUME ITEM
ORDER #53-9 Garment 7C Belted short Trench coat	ORDER #53-9 Trench Jacket Lining	trench coat buckle

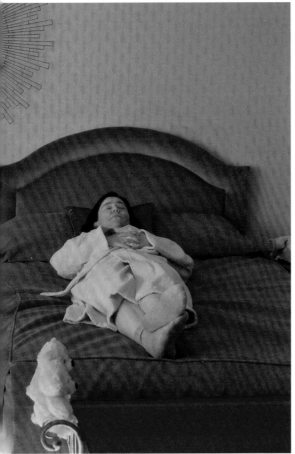

"We're on top of the world." —SUSIE

For Susie in Vegas, I introduced more and more classi- cally tailored suit vests into her costumes, both to enhance her "professional" look and to allow her to gamble in shirtsleeves from time to time without compromising her managerial image. The key was to let her get *slightly* more "classy" without losing sight of her class*ic* Susie persona.

The drag race was probably Susie's most significant Vegas adventure—and her signature leather motorcycle jacket made absolute, perfect sense here! And while Susie mimics the role of actor James Dean in this sequence overtly inspired by the "chicken run" scene in *Rebel Without a Cause*, Midge's look was partially inspired by the palette of Natalie Wood's iconic costume there—but with a belted lavender trench coat that also cries French New Wave.

CHAPTER 05

Road Mode: Miami Glam

"Now, you are gonna need a bathing suit."
—*MIDGE*

I always thought the costumes in Miami would be larger than life. Then, as I began to review the research for the period in Miami Beach, I realized that, even *in reality*, the clothes were more exaggerated than I could ever imagine! The beachwear, the hats, the wacky, eccentric straw bags had a circus-like undertone that was visually very rich and exciting, with stripes and dots and patterns creating a playfully graphic atmosphere.

On the flip side, Miami Beach in the late 1950s and '60s was a celebrity destination, and the Fontainebleau the jewel in the crown—the most famous, most luxurious hotel in Miami, notably frequented by, among others, Frank Sinatra and the Rat Pack. It was a strikingly stylish venue with a very dynamic aesthetic—American with a Caribbean twist. And it was also a prominent showcase for glamour, epitomized by the mere presence of the Fontainebleau's renowned architectural folly, the "Staircase to Nowhere"—actually to a small checkroom—whose only real purpose was to provide a theatrical set for the parades of glamorous outfits descending the stairs.

"Officially a road comic."
—LENNY

I designed Midge's arrival look to anticipate this convergence of circus and glamour. So, she makes her grand, first-time, once-in-a-lifetime entrance in an elegant, loose silk shift, hand-painted with a mélange of flowers and polka dots that suggest aquatic exotica. And her pale cream hat, the widest she'd worn to date, was built from vintage straw covered with hand-painted, handmade silk flowers in pastel pinks and greens that made me think of a cluster of sea anemones poised on an underwater ledge.

And . . . since she's arriving on the crest of a successful tour that we've only seen in its earliest phase in Las Vegas, I thought her costume should echo the superhero motif I associated previously with her first pink coat and other "coats of many colors." But since she'd never actually wear a coat in sultry Miami, I added a light silk cape to her dress—now *literally* a cape—which floats and flaps and swirls super-hero-ically behind her as she sails through the Fontainebleau's expansive lobby.

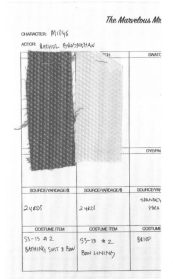

DUCK TO WATER

Unsurprisingly, Midge's first activity at the Fontainebleau after checking in is to dally by the pool, where the script initially called for her to be seen "in a super cute bathing suit, with cute hat, cute sunglasses, cute little pool heels, and a cute poolside bag full of magazines," followed by "a super cute swim hat" when she finally takes a swim. The operative word, of course, is . . . "cute!"—which I chose to interpret here as connecting Midge with her early sense of identity and aspirations. In addition, she had to stand out clearly from the carnivalesque background of extras for whom we'd built an endless assortment of beach-ball-shaped playsuits, straw bucket hats in wild colors, and varieties of patterned beach capes and coverups. For the design of her bathing suit, then, I decided to reintroduce a few signature elements from her earliest vocabulary, like the color pink and "big bow," then crowned the resulting pink, big-bowed swimsuit with a straw hat painted with pink and white fan motifs that was meant to look like a large open shell on her head.

"You should take your jacket off. You should take your boots off."
—*MIDGE*

It was more of a dilemma costuming Susie for the pool. After some initial discussions with Amy and the actress Alex Borstein, we decided that her first "swimsuit" should just consist of a pair of ragged, cut-off trousers worn with a classic white tank top and her habitual suspenders, a solution that would feel improvised, therefore quintessentially Susie. And then—serendipitously—the suspenders became a quite practical comic prop when we discovered in the pool that Midge could grip them like a harness to keep Susie afloat while teaching her to, um, dog paddle!

Then Susie's second swimsuit was more conventional, the sort of suit she might find in a hotel gift shop. Emblazoned with large blue flowers, it was designed to be comically retro—even from the perspective of 1960!

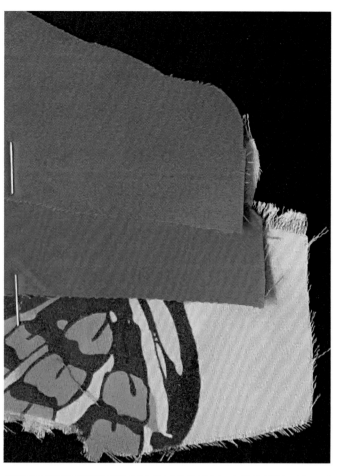

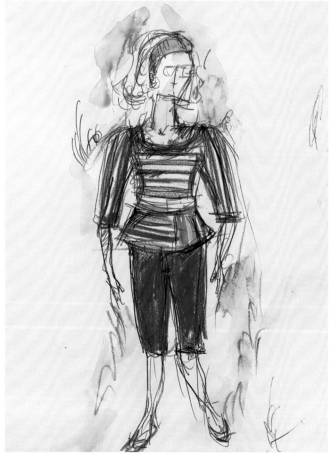

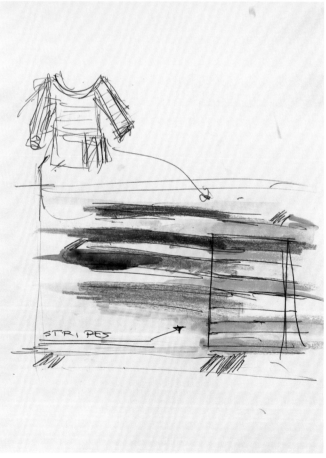

"The perfect chance to finally wear that boating outfit I brought on tour." —MIDGE

Miami by day was colorful, extroverted, and playful, with most costumes to some degree reflecting its character as a waterfront resort, and I tended to use larger, bolder patterns than usual, even for Midge. Her blue-on-pink, parrot-print dress, with its blue top and large blue straw hat, and the raspberry, multicolor-dot dress with its ribboned visor, are two perfect examples of costumes that combine playful patterns and shapes in a distinctly "Miamian" way.

Then Midge's boating look takes her from beachfront culture straight out to sea, reinterpreting the archetypal look of a Breton sailor. The combination of classic blue and white with unconventional orange stripes makes for a fanciful take on an outfit, which, in true Midge style, expressed her idea of what one *ought* to wear to fit in and yet stand out in style on a sailboat. Plenty of stripes, blue capris, and a raffia belt with an orange leather buckle—choices all worthy of a fashion-conscious swabbie!

MIAMI AFTER DARK

Miami was as glamorous by night as it was playful by day. But given her busy performance schedule, most of Midge's evening clothes were also, in fact, her "limelight" or performance looks. And although in Miami she starts to add touches of color to these dresses, they remain essentially black, like the layered fringe sheath dress she models with evident glee on the Staircase to Nowhere.

Her only other evening look was the dress she wears for her night out with Lenny, or as I like to call it, her "Lenny date dress," for which I chose a strikingly bold, pink-and-black floral pattern that I felt would be emotionally powerful, but with shoulder straps made from pink tulle for a balletic touch of lightness. This dress would be seen at the TV taping of *Miami After Dark* (an allusion, of course, to *Playboy After Dark*), at the Cuban club, Lenny's hotel, and then, after a long, basically sleepless night, by the Fontainebleau pool against the improbable backdrop of an early morning water ballet. And since this was the first *really* romantic interlude Midge shares with Lenny, it had to be memorable.

267

MIAMI LIBRE

I totally *loved* designing the costumes for the Cuban club. By the end of the 1950s, a large part of Miami's cultural landscape was already under the sway of "Latin," primarily Cuban, influence, and, with successive waves of exiles to Miami during this period—fleeing first from Batista, then from Castro—the impact of Cuban culture was at a peak.

In addition to the club's sleek and sophisticated clients, and the waiters in red shirts and boaters, I designed a

Cuban dance number initially inspired by a Russian-made film, *I Am Cuba*, that we'd watched for background research. The dancers' costumes, channeling images of tropical vegetation, were all made from simple muslin dyed to a palette of colors specifically concocted for this scene. The tall hats, like hybrids of clown and ecclesiastical headdresses, consisted of bits of fishing net and rice paper, covered with shredded raffia and beaded with large red, yellow, and orange stones. With these raw, tactile materials, I hoped to complement the rhythmic sensuality of the music and choreography, as the number sets the scene for Midge and Lenny's romantic dance.

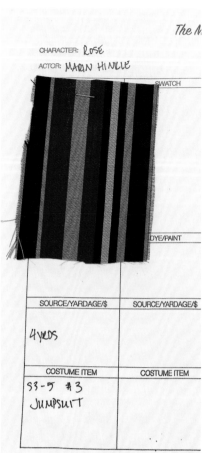

CHARACTER: ROSE
ACTOR: MARIN HINKLE

SWATCH

DYE/PAINT

SOURCE/YARDAGE/$	SOURCE/YARDAGE/$
4 YRDS	
COSTUME ITEM	COSTUME ITEM
S3-5 #3 JUMPSUIT	

"I don't have anything to wear . . ." —ROSE

Having escaped to Miami from the Maisels' house in Queens, both Abe and Rose continue to consolidate the new directions their lives are now starting to take both individually and together. Not since Paris have we seen Rose so madly eclectic and assertive in her style, and she lets herself go in Miami in ways she could never do in the Catskills under the critical eye of her peers.

For her first daytime look, I made her a striped culotte dress paired with a hat that was virtually smothered with an impressive number of brightly colored pompoms. And we first see her by night at Shy's performance in a green and white silk dress with a huge matching bow on her head, cavorting and drinking heavily as she emerges from her cocoon. Suddenly Midge seems positively ladylike and proper by comparison.

The Marvelous Mrs. Maisel

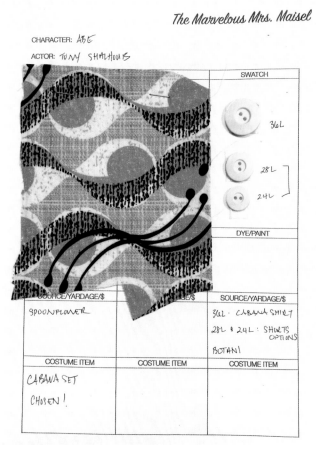

CHARACTER: ABE

ACTOR: TONY SHALHOUB

		SWATCH
		36L
		28L
		24L
		DYE/PAINT
SOURCE/YARDAGE/$	SOURCE/YARDAGE/$	SOURCE/YARDAGE/$
SPOONFLOWER		36L · CABANA SHIRT
		28L & 24L : SHORTS OPTIONS
		BOTANI
COSTUME ITEM	COSTUME ITEM	COSTUME ITEM
CABANA SET CHOSEN!		

"I wear flowered shorts to work."
—ASHER

Abe, while remaining more constant, as always, is nevertheless at his most entertaining—and characteristically quirkiest—in his diving gear and beachwear, a patterned cabana set made of vintage fabrics, which he wears to reconnect with his old playwright buddy Asher, played by Jason Alexander, a critical encounter for Abe and an omen of life to come.

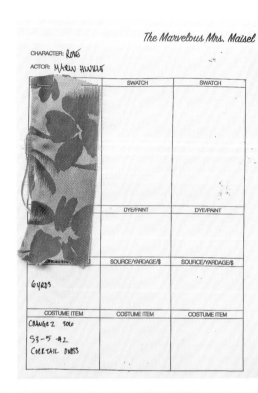

The Marvelous Mrs. Maisel

CHARACTER: ROSE
ACTOR: MARIN HINKLE

	SWATCH	SWATCH
	DYE/PAINT	DYE/PAINT
	SOURCE/YARDAGE/$	SOURCE/YARDAGE/$
6 YRDS		
COSTUME ITEM	COSTUME ITEM	COSTUME ITEM
CHANGE 2 SOLO S3-5 #2 COCKTAIL DRESS		

275

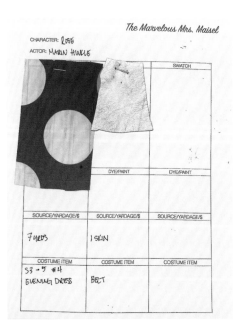

The Marvelous Mrs. Maisel

CHARACTER: ROSE

ACTOR: MARIN HINKLE

		SWATCH
DYE/PAINT	DYE/PAINT	
SOURCE/YARDAGE/$	SOURCE/YARDAGE/$	SOURCE/YARDAGE/$
7 YRDS	1 SKIN	
COSTUME ITEM	COSTUME ITEM	COSTUME ITEM
S3 → 5 #4 EVENING DRESS	BELT	

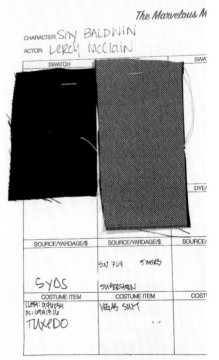

The Marvelous M

CHARACTER: Shy BALDWIN
ACTOR: LeROY McClain

SWATCH		SWA
		DYE/
SOURCE/YARDAGE/$	SOURCE/YARDAGE/$	SOURCE/
	5N 708 5 YARDS	
SYDS	SUPERSHEEN	
COSTUME ITEM	COSTUME ITEM	COST
CLOTH: 0176084 PC: 09.17.16	VEGAS SUIT	
TUXEDO		

CHAPTER 06

Class & Sass on Broadway

"This is a classy f------ play!"
—SUSIE

Onstage and off, Sophie Lennon is Midge's nemesis, the proverbial *anti-Midge*, and her abrasive, artificial stage persona Sophie from Queens is the antithesis of the captivating, genuine Mrs. Maisel.

Equally artificial, but poles apart in her offstage life—more like Sophie from Fifth Avenue!—Sophie lives, dresses, and comports herself like a diva. Surrounded by her imposing Russian wolfhounds and an obsequious staff of butlers and other "menservants," her bearing and behavior are virtually impossible to reconcile with vulgar, fat-suited Sophie from Queens. And so, for Sophie's private moments, I often dressed her in flowing, kimono-shaped garments or capes, cloche hats and turbans, and dramatic, silver "art brut" jewelry chosen for its powerfully graphic look.

Susie's sporadic encounters with Sophie often take unexpected turns, like leaving Sophie's mansion in one of her cast-off fur coats, replicating the dénouement of Midge's prior visit in season one. In both cases, I used period furs I found in the vintage stock of a New York furrier, the challenge being to locate coats that might credibly be expected to fit the character played by actress Jane Lynch, who is quite tall, and yet still be worn by Midge or Susie if only for comic effect.

Then, in a sudden shift, with Susie as her new manager and resentful of Midge, Sophie decides to validate herself as a "serious" actress by taking on the title role in August Strindberg's tragic *Miss Julie*.

We first see Gavin, her prospective leading man, played by Cary Elwes, in an amusing backstage dressing room scene with Susie, still wearing his costume and makeup from a performance of *Macbeth*, and I liberally interpreted his costume by mixing multiple plaids and linens, doused with generous quantities of stage blood to heighten the comic impact of their otherwise routine negotiations.

Then, for Gavin's scenes with Sophie in the rehearsal hall, I modeled his look on images of dancer-choreographers like Gene Kelly, with typically loose gabardine shirts and silk ascots. And, as rehearsals progressed, I had him wear a deconstructed, late nineteenth-century jacket covered with basting stitches, his costume for *Miss Julie* as a work in progress, seen in various stages of development— a sleeve on, a sleeve off, no sleeves at all!—as we close in on opening night.

"Tonight, Miss Julie is crazy again. Absolutely crazy."
—*GAVIN, IN* MISS JULIE

To help her to get into character, Sophie's rehearsal clothes were simplified versions of late nineteenth-century bustle skirts built in black, polished Dutch linen, combined with her own contemporary 1950s deep-toned knit tops and signature silver jewelry.

282

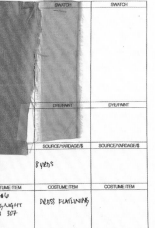

SWATCH	SWATCH
DYE/PAINT	DYE/PAINT
SOURCE/YARDAGE/$	SOURCE/YARDAGE/$
8 YRDS	
COSTUME ITEM	COSTUME ITEM
DRESS FLATLINING	

Then, for her Miss Julie costume, the episode's *pièce de résistance*, I wanted to create an impression of cascading ruffles and stripes that would be beautiful to look at while still harboring a hidden potential for humor. In the end, it was cut to an authentic 1880s pattern and built from a medley of cottons and silks to suggest a patchwork of Swedish-inspired blue-and-white stripes in varying proportions. And these elegant, but moderately exaggerated stripes on the dress were designed to coordinate comically with the ticking on the pillow Sophie ultimately dons for stomach padding when her character uncontrollably reverts from Miss Julie back into Sophie from Queens.

For Gavin and Moira, the other two actors in the play, we also built historically accurate costumes, but in muted tones, mainly black and white, to keep the focus on Sophie and provide a more neutral background for her dramatically striped ensemble.

Midge had come to the theater to see Sophie's show in one of her most evocative pink looks, a deep raspberry silk dress inspired by late 1950s couture, and Susie sports what are now indispensable elements of her "serious" managerial look, a tailored suit jacket and vest. We last see them after the show outside the theater in angry confrontation with Sophie, who is still in her costume—and pillow! She is literally coming apart, with her improvised padding on public display, an image that effectively sums up the folly of the whole venture.

CHAPTER 07

Clothes at Work: Piecework Threads

"This game is piecework. You do a lot, you make a lot."
—*DICKIE*

After her inaugural tour with Shy is cut short right after Miami by Shy's recovery from "exhaustion," we find Midge pursuing a day job for the second time in the series. But while her previous stint at B. Altman was a basically *regular* full-time job, Midge is now steered by Susie through a highly *irregular* whirlwind series of radio spots produced at a frenzied pace. So making sure that the clothes would stay in sync with the sheer momentum of the scenes was a major concern in their design.

Everything in the episode was built for movement—and for moving quickly! In their frantic race from one studio to another, we frequently see the overbooked duo in transit—on the subway, on the street, in and out of taxis—sometimes laden with insanely ridiculous "payments in kind" for Midge's "services rendered," like the comically oversize boxes of tampons, or—indignity of indignities!—pancake syrup.

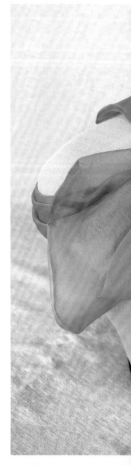

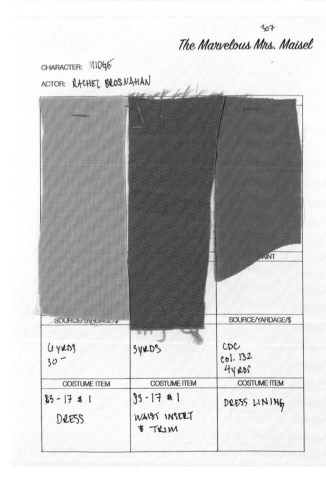

307

The Marvelous Mrs. Maisel

CHARACTER: MIDGE

ACTOR: RACHEL BROSNAHAN

SOURCE/YARDAGE/$		SOURCE/YARDAGE/$
4 YRDS 30-	3 YRDS	CDC col. 132 4 YRDS
COSTUME ITEM	**COSTUME ITEM**	**COSTUME ITEM**
83-17 #1 DRESS	83-17 #1 WAIST INSERT & TRIM	DRESS LINING

"It's f------ radio. It doesn't matter how you look." —SUSIE

And although this meant that Midge was still performing in some way, her voice-over work for radio was worlds apart from a live performance onstage in front of an audience. In her radio days, she is not onstage and therefore not effectively "Mrs. Maisel." But if a principal source of irony in these scenes, as Susie points out, is that clothes-conscious Midge is now obliged to perform without being seen, that fact remains totally inconsequential to Midge, who still needs to color her world to keep it relevant. While Midge once basically tried her best to assimilate at B. Altman, she has since become even pluckier and more confident, and so, for her radio gigs, she just brazenly flaunts her colorful style in a working world that's indifferent to appearances.

"Housewife?" —MIDGE

"What else?" —DICKIE

Midge was in a state of suspension while waiting for Shy to recuperate, but I wanted to affirm her unflinching resolve in embracing this interim with a positive outlook and humor. And because it was also the season of rejuvenation—springtime!—I decided to work with a crisp pastel palette of cleansing, fresh colors to celebrate her spirit of renewal.

I began her radio exploits with her heroic color, green, and her first "piecework" costume, still affected by the Miami aesthetic, was, even by New York standards, offbeat. Like her Miami arrival look, it was inspired by somewhat abstract, subaqueous images of sea anemones— a bottomless source of inspiration for me—and the ensemble was a lime and seafoam suit topped with a hat made from wildly twisted lengths of transparent blue and sea green organza. The hat alone, I thought, would make a splash on a crowded New York City subway!

Then Midge's second radio look, which also makes a comically incongruous appearance on the subway, was a pale baby blue suit with a canary yellow pillbox. And, like the previous costume, it was meant to project enough silliness and girlish appeal to instill some freshness and humor into the hard-edged ambiance of the commercial recording studios, a tough-as-nails environment of unforgiving employers.

"Step up to the mic and say the words. Then I will buy you a hat." —SUSIE

Midge wore her last "piecework threads" at the Maisels' house in Queens for her nephew's bris, then to her final gig, a live radio spot for the odious Phyllis Schlafly, whose barely concealed racist message provoked an unforeseen crisis of conscience for Midge. So, to stress the inherent conflict between her character and the content of the broadcast, I found a truly incredible piece of fabric with a pattern of red poppies that would help her appear even more at odds with its context.

And because this last spot was one of the most politically charged moments of the series, I hoped, by dressing Midge in a whimsical dress of narcotic red flowers, to assert my belief in the power of a costume being wonderfully *inap-*propriate to heighten the tension or conflict of a scene.

CHAPTER 08

Over the (Pink) Moon: The Apollo

"I'm feeling a little nostalgic."
—MIDGE

Rachel once surprised me by saying the navy blue and pink outfit she wears as Midge to revisit her old apartment in season three was actually one of her favorite looks in the series.

Because of the way the outfit weaves her past, present, and future together, I'd drawn largely on the vocabulary of her early, more vulnerable looks—the schoolgirl motif for the silhouette and details, and the color pink for trim, but superimposed on a dark navy blue that's meant to give it gravitas, especially when combined with its matching, navy blue wide-brimmed hat.

And in fact, that scene precipitates the chain of events that lead to Midge's triumph in recovering her now once and future home, where later, after performing at the Apollo, we see her euphorically twirling through the empty rooms in her luxurious, pink-on-pink Apollo coat.

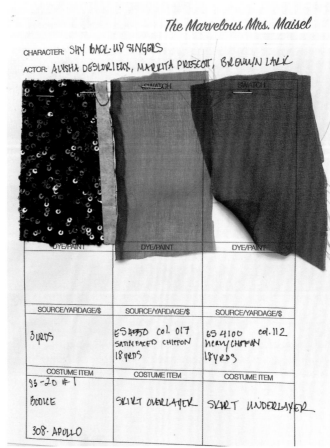

The Marvelous Mrs. Maisel

CHARACTER: SHY BACL: UP SINGERS

ACTOR: ALYSHA DESLORIEUX, MARITA PRESCOTT, BRENNYN LARK

DYE/PAINT	DYE/PAINT	DYE/PAINT
SOURCE/YARDAGE/$	SOURCE/YARDAGE/$	SOURCE/YARDAGE/$
3 YRDS	ES4750 col. 017 SATIN FACED CHIFFON 18 YRDS	ES 4100 col. 112 HEAVY CHIFFON 18 YRDS
COSTUME ITEM	COSTUME ITEM	COSTUME ITEM
S3-20 #1 BODICE 308 - APOLLO	SKIRT OVERLAYER	SKIRT UNDERLAYER

APOLLO TO THE MOON

The Apollo Theater, due to its central role in Harlem's entertainment history, was, and remains, one of the most iconic theater venues in New York City, and Midge's appearance there with Shy for the kickoff concert of their European tour is in fact her first performance ever in a large-scale variety "palace." Elegant and upscale, but with a strong community feeling, it's also the scene of Shy's comeback, and, because it's on his own home turf in Harlem, Midge sees it as the most challenging, daunting venue in their travels together to date. And so, maybe to boost her courage, she interrupts her succession of black performance looks with a super study in pink, her most elaborate limelight look to date and an echo of her first impromptu performance at the Gaslight.

The Marvelous Mrs. Maisel

CHARACTER: MOMS MABLEY

ACTOR: WANDA SYKES

SOURCE/YARDAGE		RDAGE/$
2 YRDS	5 YRDS	1.5 YRD
COSTUME ITEM	COSTUME ITEM	COSTUME ITEM
DRESS COLLAR + CUFFS	DRESS	HAT

"Geez. That's not intimidating at all."
—*MIDGE*

The program at the Apollo consisted of music, dance, and comedy numbers, with the fictional Shy Baldwin on the marquee with real-life stars like the tap-dancing Hines Brothers and, most essential to the narrative, Jackie "Moms" Mabley, played by Wanda Sykes. Like Lenny Bruce, Moms was a real person, who had first played the Apollo in 1939 and was one of the most renowned stand-up comics of the era, so her costume was very much influenced by historical research.

Throughout the years, Moms's performance look, like her stage persona, was constant and specific—a boldly patterned, cotton print housedress, house slippers, argyle socks, and a bell-shaped knit hat—a version of which we actually did hand-knit! In research photos, I noticed that one of her trademark dresses was made from a pineapple print, which I loved, but considered too impractical to produce because of the pattern. Then, in one of those exhilarating moments when solutions can appear as if by magic, we found a perfect swatch of a perfect fabric in a perfect weight (!)—and were soon on our way to creating a perfect take on the original!

"I thought I'd go understated today . . ."
—*MIDGE*

When their paths do cross backstage at the Apollo, Moms and Midge couldn't look more incompatible. Like Sophie Lennon, Moms belongs to a vaudeville tradition in which women can only be funny when they are frumpy and unglamorous, although unlike Sophie, Moms's persona is genuine and sincere.

Midge, on the other hand, revels in glamour, and her Apollo dress, with its oversized bow, was her most ornate, extravagant performance look to date. It was built from a very special piece of silk, then hand-embroidered with beads and sequins, exceeding all of her previous limelight looks in terms of embellishment. It was a peak of decorative pink—Midge's pinnacle of pinkness—as if we were rolling all of her prior pink moments, with all their accumulated effects, into one great *SHOUT* of pink—one glorious, rousing crescendo!

The Marvelous Mrs. Maisel

CHARACTER: MIDGE
ACTOR: RACHEL BROSNAHAN

SWATCH

SWATCH

DYE/PAINT

DYE/PAINT

"Welcome home."
—MIDGE

Establishing the pink
through line for this
sequence, Midge arrives in
a whirlwind at the Apollo in
an intensely pink-on-pink,
deep pink on light pink silk
coat, which largely masks
her performance dress
until she reveals it to Shy in
his dressing room. The coat
was constructed using the
kind of two-dimensional,
"straight-line-cut" tech-
nique often used for Asian
traditional garments like
kimonos, which facilitated
the kind of loose, raptur-
ous, swirling movement
that accompanies Midge's
arrival at the Apollo, then
her ecstatic run through
the empty apartment on
Riverside Drive that night.

"It's 'cause I wore the wrong shoes, right?"
—MIDGE

The last scene on the tarmac, Midge and Susie's disheartening face-off with Reggie, ultimately concludes the Apollo sequence, and the season, on a very poignant note. Midge, having begun her departure in Queens with joy and confidence, her myriad pieces of luggage filled with myriad hopes and dreams—and myriad changes of clothing!—now suddenly crumples in the wake of her abrupt termination from the tour.

Each season featured at least one major emotional transition using an off-white costume as a refrain, like the cream white coat Midge wears to bail Lenny from jail at the end of the pilot, or her "All Alone" look at the end of season two—each instance signaling a new blank page, a new direction. And here, on the tarmac for the season three finale, even Susie's look was "creamy," with a new jacket reminiscent of the vintage white dinner jacket she wore in the Catskills.

And for Midge, with whom we are always looking forward, I designed an ivory white suit and bucket hat that were deliberately meant to push her silhouette into the early 1960s. It was her final outfit of the season and a parting song, less a reflection of the vanishing 1950s than a harbinger of the '60s—and the madly marvelous future of the show!

AFTERWORD

by Rachel Brosnahan

Donna Zakowska is literally the Mad Hatter of *The Marvelous Mrs. Maisel*, and to be outfitted by her is both a dream and a delight.

It cannot be overstated how much I enjoy our fittings. They are often the first interaction I have with a new script after reading it (and sometimes even before I've received it!), and an opportunity to see the world of the show through Donna's eyes. Whether we're at Eric Winterling's studio (where Midge's clothes are beautifully constructed) or the costume shop at Steiner Studios, the space is littered with reference photos, sketches, colorful swatches, and what feels like an endless supply of shoes, hats, jewelry, and gloves to try with the various looks. Donna expertly breathes new life into textures, patterns, fabrics, and silhouettes, and it sometimes feels as though she's added new colors to the rainbow. The collaboration between Donna, Eric, our milliner Lynne Mackey, our corsetière Emmanuelle Poignan, all of the dressers, assistants, and craftswomen and men who work to bring these clothes to life is nothing short of inspiring. I often feel like Cinderella watching these stunning clothes magically materialize around me, but it is thanks to the shorthand between the teams at work and the many hours of careful construction that I get to live my own 1950s princess fantasy. Every fitting, despite the long shoot days that nearly always precede it, is imbued with a vitality and exuberance that reenergize and carry us into each next chapter.

Watching Donna work is a masterclass. She is meticulous in every aspect of her craft from research to design to execution, from background to day players to series regulars, from selecting on-set dressers to her closest collaborators. She's a powerful storyteller and world builder and deeply understands the emotional arc of each and every character and how their clothes reflect or protect their inner life. She is a bold and brilliant leader who demands excellence from everyone around her, and is also a true collaborator who works openly and honestly with each department to make our show leap to life. Upon first meeting with Donna, I knew three things were true: that she knew this character better than I did; that we were kindred spirits; and that working together would be one of the greatest privileges of my life and career. All three remain true today.

303

Editor: Meredith A. Clark
Managing Editor: Mike Richards
Designer: Diane Shaw
Design Manager: Jenice Kim
Production Manager: Rachael Marks

Library of Congress Control Number:
2021932561

ISBN: 978-1-4197-4441-9
eISBN: 978-1-64700-472-9

Printed and bound in China
10 9 8 7 6 5 4 3 2 1

Abrams books are available at special
discounts when purchased in quantity
for premiums and promotions as well
as fundraising or educational use. Special
editions can also be created to specifica-
tion. For details, contact specialsales@
abramsbooks.com or the address below.

Abrams® is a registered trademark of
Harry N. Abrams, Inc.

ABRAMS The Art of Books
195 Broadway, New York, NY 10007
abramsbooks.com